CHRISTIAN COLLEGE LIBRARY
COLUMBIA, MISSOURI
WITHDRAWN

D1482963

¶ BY BILL VAUGHAN

Sorry I Stirred It

Bird Thou Never Wert

SORRY
I STIRRED IT

With a Preface
Foreword
Introduction
Epilogue
One Illustration
and
Several Decorations by

BILL VAUGHAN

Hereinafter Referred to as The Author

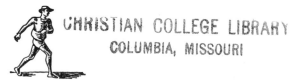

CHRISTIAN COLLEGE LIBRARY
COLUMBIA, MISSOURI

Simon and Schuster : New York
1964

ACKNOWLEDGMENT

¶ Much of this material first appeared in the Kansas City *Star*. It has been assembled with the feeling that any voices rising from the Middle West had better be recorded in more or less permanent form before everybody moves to one coast or the other.

All rights reserved
including the right of reproduction
in whole or in part in any form
Copyright © 1962, 1963, 1964 by Bill Vaughan
Published by Simon and Schuster, Inc.
Rockefeller Center, 630 Fifth Avenue
New York 20, N. Y.

FIRST PRINTING

Library of Congress Catalog Card Number: 64–17504
Manufactured in the United States of America
By H. Wolff, New York

22866

817.54
V465s

To
Daisy *and/or* Lenore.

CONTENTS

Under the new leisure: more time to work ¶ Two for the slant bar ¶ The check that whispers, "Someone insolvent has passed by" ¶ Dial your way to mental health ¶ Did Edison feel like a filament? ¶ If it's worth doing, it's worth deducting ¶ Psst! a copy of "Tropic of Corporation"? ¶ Economics, a shirt-sleeve science ¶ Can a nation survive without adjectives? ¶ The folksy bank bakes its own bread ¶ Do we need an image subsidy?

If a disease is worth having it's worth supporting ¶ Even the conversation is catered ¶ It's smart to live in the past if you sell souvenirs ¶ Who's that out there serenading my aspidistra? ¶ Will success spoil culture? ¶ They don't make monsters like King Kong any more ¶ A man is known by the scapegoats he keeps ¶ "I don't know if this will help, officer, but he looked like a whole man to me" ¶ We never sang folk songs because my folks weren't folk ¶ Reverse

Motorist, put me back ¶ *I can remember stuff I never even heard of* ¶ *She called me typical, but she smiled* ¶ *It was a real pleasure to put your book down* ¶ *One thing about snobbishness, it keeps you young* ¶ *My last exclusive . . .* ¶ *A man has to keep his bubble vulcanized* ¶ *Windows or science: which?* ¶ *The trouble corn can cause*

EPILOGUE   186

PREFACE

¶ *Waiter:* How is the soup, sir?
Customer: I'm sort of sorry I stirred it.
—FOLK JOKE

Jean Kerr, the lady who takes the bread out of the mouth of the workingman by writing funny, said one time on television, when I happened to be watching it, that "I'm sorry I stirred it" was a favorite phrase of her husband's to express regret for getting involved in any complicated enterprise which might have been avoided.

She attributed it to a real-life incident related by Howard Lindsay. Frank Sullivan, on the other hand, says it came from a musical comedy featuring Harry Watson.

My own feeling is that it is a joke we have always had with us. Waiter-customer jokes may be the oldest form of humor.

Is there anywhere in the English-speaking world anyone who cannot give the second line to such openers as:

Customer: "My cocoa is cold."
Customer: "There's a fly in my soup."
Waiter: "It looks like rain."
Customer: "Do you serve crabs?"
?

(In this kind of thing where do you put the question mark? I let it stand, just above, waiting to be assigned. It is the sort of grammatical construction that makes you wish you hadn't stirred it.)

Whatever its origin, "I'm sorry I stirred it" is a phrase which occurs to the writer for the daily press who is awakened at 2 A.M. by calls such as one I will always remember. It was a lady, inquiring indignantly, "Who do you think you are, making fun of King Farouk, who has done more for Egypt than you ever have?"

Here and there in this book I have tried to indicate a few things that perhaps I shouldn't have stirred. Some others may occur to the sensitive reader.

FOREWORD

¶ Women are the people who think if there's a cherry in it, it's not intoxicating, and if you charge it, it doesn't cost anything.

¶ The trouble with the average family is it has too much month left over at the end of the money.

¶ A henpecked man is one who smokes a big, black cigar while doing the dishes in an effort to show that he isn't.

These are what I understand are known in some circles as aphorisms. In newspapers they are called paragraphs and I have been, for eighteen years, a paragrapher. (Put the emphasis on whatever syllable you prefer. Although I know that a paragrapher is what I am, I have never been called it to my face so I am hazy about the pronunciation.)

I have written a conservatively estimated 95,000 paragraphs under various names and pseudonyms, including that of the syndicated Senator Soaper. I quote the three above merely because they are all at least fifteen years old and seem to be immortal. They keep turning up, attributed to Anon. and other authors. Not that I mind it. I have been long enough in the business to know that nobody ever really said anything first.

A while back a horse fell on the ice in Kansas City and nobody knew how to get her up. It saddened me. Every town used to have a paragrapher and a man who knew how to get horses up off the ice.

One discipline, apparently, has died out, and mine may be right behind it. It is for this reason that I have sprinkled a few paragraphs through this book. In memoriam, perhaps, of a craft that has included Kin Hubbard and Benjamin Franklin, Franklin P. Adams, Harry Wade, Luke McLuke and several Frenchmen.

Out of 95,000 paragraphs a man who has never kept files cannot make an intelligent sampling, much less a choice of the best (or least bad). The paragraphs in this book have been reconstituted, but I am pretty sure that, sometime, I have written something very similar to them.

INTRODUCTION

When some perceptive social critic rears back and hurls a javelin at our American preoccupation with bigness, I can't help but sympathize. Over the years that I have spent in writing small paragraphs of humorous intent, I have run into old friends whose invariable opening remark is "Are you still writing those little squibs for the paper?"

"Why, yes," I am tempted to reply, if the interrogator is an obstetrician. "Are you still bringing those little tiny people into the world?"

Innate courtesy forbids me to do more than counter with some such pleasantry as "Go climb a rope."

It takes considerable restraint. Surely I would be justified in answering, in the case of a professional golfer, "Are you still hitting that little ball? I'd have thought you'd be up to hitting at least volleyballs by now."

What we must do is realize that the world needs men who think and work small as well as those who think and work big.

I had a grandfather who carved peach seeds into little monkeys. He explained to me once that you looked at the peach seed and if you could see a little monkey in there, then all you had to do was carve off the rest of the peach seed.

This principle is a familiar one to sculptors. Gutzon Borglum, for example, looked at Mount Rushmore and saw Washington and Lincoln and Teddy Roosevelt and who knows who all in there. He went to work and blasted and chiseled until he got them out of that granite prison, or part way out anyway.

Now the world will make value judgments and say that Gutzon Borglum was a greater man than my grandfather, and maybe the world is right. What I object to is that if you press the world as to how it arrived at that conclusion, it is likely to say, "Well, Gutzon Borglum's got an ear on Abraham Lincoln there that would hold two bushels of your grandfather's peach stones."

All I say about Gutzon Borglum and my grandfather (who, incidentally, never met) is that they were different men. One carved small, the other big.

My grandfather was plagued all his life by people saying, "Hey, Doc, you still carving those little peach seeds?"

People might have asked Borglum, "Hey, Gutzon, you still carving those little mountains?" and taunted him because he didn't go carve Everest. But I doubt if they did. Rushmore may not be big as mountains go, but those are still awfully big statues.

My Muse, a large and Rubenesque lady, has visited my chambers, lit up one of my cigars, and said, "Sam, baby, you'll never hack it with those little squibs."

She has pointed out to me more than once that poundage is what counts in the culture game.

"When you get up to Mount Olympus, Sam," she has told me, "the first thing you'll find is a scale. You got to weigh in. The heavier the product the higher the pillow. Paragraphers sleep on the wine-dark floor along with the poets.

"The thing for you to do is write a novel or a series of eight interlocking novels presenting the entire panorama of civilization, Sam, where you got to read the last one to understand the first.

"Or collect an anthology of other people's stuff, which is probably the easiest work per pound.

"The point is you can't niggle your way through life."

Well, like any Muse, she knows the business, and I'm leaving out the fact that she'd understandably rather have 10 per cent of a book that tears the roof off the Department of Commerce and tells the lusty, fast-paced story of passion and intrigue underneath same, to say nothing of the movie money, than to work with a niggler where the best you can get is maybe ten bucks per niggle for reprint rights from the *Reader's Digest*.

She is probably right, and I occasionally swing for the long

a. *Comparative size of Mount Rushmore sculpture and peach stone monkey*

b. *Comparative size of Gutzon Borglum and my grandfather*

ball. I have, on occasion and without oxygen, hit 900 or 1,000 words.

And, in doing so, I'm not being disloyal to my grandfather. Every so often he used to go down to Florida and carve a coconut.

¶ BETWEEN COFFEE BREAKS,
I HEAR AMERICA WORKING

Relaxing in a commodious airplane seat the other morning, sipping the compulsory breakfast champagne, I remarked, in an urbane manner, to the adjoining gentleman, "Who you with, Mac?"

Well, it turned out his name was Gridley and he used to live around Smackover, Arkansas, in case I knew anybody down there, which I don't, but I said I had heard of Clyde Scott, who was from there before he played football.

The big news, however, was that he was vice-president of the Intime Watch Company.

"Maybe you can help me out then, Mac," I said, detaching my watch and handing it to him. "This thing don't keep a bit of good time. I think, speaking just as a layman, that the trouble is probably when I had it fixed last they didn't have a Mickey Mouse arm to put on for the hour hand and they had to use a Porky Pig leg. Just a lay opinion, of course, and I would be glad for you to stick the old loupe in your eye and give me the expert word."

"I would like to help you out, friend," he retorted courteously, "but what I know about watches I could stick in my eye right along with the loupe, whatever that may be."

"How then?" I queried.

"I am with the tomato sauce branch of the Gourmet Foods Division of the Intime Watch Company. From vine to kettle to can, the tomato is my responsibility," he said, with perhaps pardonable pride.

"You surprise me," I remarked, "that the Intime Watch Company makes tomato sauce."

"Oh," he said with perhaps pardonable modesty, "the tomato sauce branch, indeed the entire Gourmet Foods Division, is only a small facet of our complex. It is not, for example, nearly as big even as our insecticide operation. Then, too, we make seat covers, shingles, lamp shades, golf clubs, outboard motors, chinaware, masking tape and a complete line of power tools for the home handyman. This, of course, in addition to our life insurance branch, the travel agency and the underwater oil exploration subsidiary."

"You forgot the watches," I reminded him.

He took a reflective sip of his champagne and commented parenthetically, "An excellent champagne. I know the people that make it—the Kackefuss Brothers, heavy construction and bridge contractors of Kennebunk, Maine."

After another sip, he added, "They took over the champagne line when the Camden and Ong's Hat Railroad, which had wholly owned it, decided to switch to a stylish-stout swimsuit operation which the Amalgamated Tobacco Company had been conducting without much success in Eau Claire.

"But forgive me. You inquired about the watches. I'm pretty sure something was said about them at the last executive committee meeting, but if it was whether we were or weren't still making them I'm not sure. It's an interesting point. I'll check on it when I get back to HQ."

It turns out that the only surprising thing about this conversation is that it should have surprised me. I seem to be the last one in my circle of acquaintances to have absorbed the word that hardly any company today is in the line of business that you might think.

This is known as diversification, and I'm glad I found out about it, even belatedly. Imagine how embarrassing it would be to walk into the main plant of the Acme Mop Works and say brightly to the receptionist, "Well, lovely one, how does the mop flop today?"

And it would turn out they are making nose cones or harmonicas or beer.

Now that I understand corporate diversification, I find life more interesting. When I discovered one of the children needed a bicycle, I thought I would try to get one wholesale, so I took a chance and called the brother-in-law of an old friend.

This fellow works for the Orbital Space Products and Electronic Components, Inc. For some reason they don't make bicycles, but he fixed me up over at the Phaedo Dog Food plant, where they do. And the nice guy at Orbital gave me a good price on a set of matched leather luggage.

Under the new leisure: more time to work

Machines are showing up in various offices and factories and are getting a rather chilly reception.

Like people will say to an electronic brain, "Look, I was working for this company when your grandfather was handing out candy bars for a nickel in the slot."

Lots of us are afraid that a machine will take over our job, and there are all sorts of shock waves beating upon highly placed eardrums. The point is that nobody is really in favor of a machine coming in and taking the bread out of the workingman's mouth.

Yet, there is the other side of it. Many widows and orphans and senior citizens have their money in automation stocks. It can't just be called off.

What strikes me is that we are training these machines the wrong way. We are developing them to do good, productive work which, as everyone knows, is what people are here for. It is what we learn from parent, church and school. When it comes to an honest day's endeavor, I'll take men or women in preference to machines every time.

But there are a lot of us flesh-and-bloods who are wasting our time in other activities. Here is where the plug-in folks could be a big help.

Take in the average company where many a man has to go to protracted lunches and hear talks on "The Challenge at the Crossroads." Why not send the machines to do that? It should be child's play for our scientists to develop a machine that could drink two martinis and applaud every five minutes.

Or, if an out-of-town client is around, why should he be taken to the night spots by a human being? Let an electronic brain show him around.

The client, of course, would have to trundle the machine into the nightclub and plug him in, but after that he would be as good, or better, than a real person. A tape recording would spout sophisticated conversation, electric eyes would scan the photographs of the client's wife and children, and a credit card would be emitted from a convenient slot when the check came.

For that matter, the client's company could send a machine. Then one machine could entertain the other. The cab driver could lug them in, the headwaiter would hitch up the electrical current and they could entertain each other all evening.

Look at the way we waste so much of our most priceless resource by having our youths hang around the street corners. Any reliable statistician will tell you that we waste 37 billion dollars a year, or any other figure you may require, by having our youths hanging around street corners.

Doesn't it make more sense to have a battery of machines hanging around the street corners?

For a mere fraction of what it costs us to man the street corners of America with real, live youths, we can have machines there, whistling at the girls and creating an occasional disturbance.

I know a man who is a terrific bookkeeper but a terrible fisherman. The crazy way things are headed now, they will replace him with a machine that won't do half as good a job of bookkeeping and leave him free to do this fiddle-footed fishing of his, with falling out of the boat and putting hooks in other people and all the rest.

It seems so much more reasonable to keep the man on the job and let a machine do the fishing. Efficient, silent, safe fishing machines can certainly be developed.

In other words, let's have the machines take over all the

expensive, wasteful, uneconomic leisure time of America and let people keep on doing the work.

¶ Automation is a threat, of course. But being replaced by a machine isn't nearly as humiliating as being replaced by a son-in-law.

Two for the slant bar

Now that I have some stationery that says "From the Desk of . . ." I am prepared to drop a line to anybody who might like to hear from my desk and am equipped with all the trappings of success in the business jungle except the one that is perhaps the most important.

I don't have a secretary.

I haven't the slightest idea what I would do with a secretary if I had one. It's just that all the other fellows have them.

You don't know what it does to a man, viscerally, when somebody sighs at lunch, "I don't know what I would do without my Miss Overdrive. She knows more about the business than I do."

And another fellow chips in with "Yas, I know what you mean. My Miss Clambroth is a tower of strength."

Then they look at you and expect you to say something about your Miss Whatever. All you can do is mumble that the hominy *suprême* looks unusually good today.

I meet a man of some importance and he suggests that we get together on a matter to our mutual benefit.

"Have your girl," he says, "phone mine and concretize the finalities."

So when I call his girl I have to say, "This is Mr. Vaughan's girl and you'll have to excuse me, dearie, I have this terrible chest cold that is giving me a huskiness voicewise."

It is destructive of dignity.

People telephone me, or rather their secretaries do. The

secretary is naturally offended when she gets me on the telephone instead of a secretary.

The idea of a man just barefacedly and brazenly answering a telephone strikes the tenderly nurtured secretary as obscene. I try to laugh it off and explain that my girl, who usually answers the telephone, is out for coffee, ha and ha.

It doesn't go over. She knows right away that her boss is communicating with some sort of shady character from the nether world where people talk to people right on the telephone without any secretaries to chaperon them.

Then there is the matter of letters. The cachet here is the little wampus in the lower left-hand corner, where it says: JB/tr. Those initials, chastely separated by the bundling board, or slant bar, or whatever it is called, is a status symbol way out ahead of the key to the executives' washroom.

In earlier times when I had giddy dreams of glory, I used to fake it. I would write "BV/jk" or "BV/gh," but I outgrew the habit, and in the future I intend to abandon any other pretense. I don't have a secretary. It's nothing to be ashamed of. Daniel Boone didn't have a secretary.

It's nothing to be ashamed of, true. But it does give a man a pang, being left out, a stranger pressing his nose against the frosted glass of the executive suite, knowing that there is no one to share a slant bar with him.

¶ The really status-conscious executive will sprinkle his lapel with perfume before going home rather than confess to his wife that he doesn't have a secretary.

One of the more sensational charges brought against Attorney General Kennedy was that he brought his dog Brumus to work with him at the Justice Department. Contradictorily, at about the same time, sociologists were complaining that the trouble with suburbia's children was that they had never seen

Daddy at work. They had never gone to the office and operated the typewriter or the drop forge or the candy machine. They don't really know what Daddy does for a living.

My experience is that whatever goes for a child goes double, or maybe triple, for a dog.

I have often noticed that my city dogs behave very much like what I read about suburban children; they treat me, their daddy image, with contempt or, at best, an icy politeness. They seem to expect everything in the way of costly canned food and high-priced veterinary care. Never having earned one, they do not know the value of a dollar.

It seems to me that Robert F. Kennedy may have shown the way to the rest of us dog-daddy images. And if he faced ridicule and base partisan howls, I salute him all the more for his courage.

Our dogs need to know where the bones come from. They should be taken to the office so they can see that life is not all eating and lying in front of the fireplace or the air conditioner, according to the season.

We might well turn Brumus into a verb, as "to brumus," meaning "to take the dogs, children, parakeets and other household pets to watch Father work."

The check that whispers, "Someone insolvent has passed by"

A friend in the banking trade tells me of a check that went through his mill a while back. It was a company check from a perfume manufacturer and was a lovely negotiable instrument, with scrolls and flowers and pastel tints—and was, of course, impregnated by one of the more haunting scents produced by the firm that uttered it.

Before the name of the payee, it said, "Pay to the Odor of," and the amount was given as "Forty-four wonderful dollars." Even the date was the "17th Glorious Day of April."

The friend in the banking trade thought this all came on a little strong, and I am inclined to agree with him.

Still, I wonder if there shouldn't be a little more room on our checks for the expression of editorial opinion. The writing of a check—for most of us, anyway—is an emotional experience. But little of that emotion is expressed on the check itself.

I am not familiar enough with the banking laws to know just how far it could be carried. But surely a little humanizing wouldn't hurt.

There are times when we might find therapeutic release in dating a check "The 10th of a black, black February" and making it out for "Seventy-six grudging dollars" and payable to "the Avarice of" whomever we had in mind.

Why must we be so cold about it when we pay our income tax? We might write the amount as "One thousand, eight hundred and six Grateful for the Opportunity to Live in this Great Country dollars." And after our signature a little P.S.: "I wish it were more."

For the daughter at college: "Sixty-five absolutely final dollars."

When paying the rent to a landlord who is saving on the heat bills: "One hundred and twenty-five frozen dollars."

Just one adverb after our signature would breathe life into the most routine check. If we are wondering whether there is going to be enough money to cover the thing, zest would be added to the transaction if we followed our name with "hopefully," "apprehensively" or even "foolhardily."

Another thing, some of the big outfits which, from time to time, send me small amounts of money print the word EXACTLY in front of the figure. I don't hold it against the president of the company or the comptroller or whoever signs the thing. I know its all done by some electronic brain.

An electronic brain's idea of a big laugh is to send you a check for $1.87 and print "Exactly" in front of it, in big capital letters. The pretext is that this is done to keep you from raising the check to $11.87 or worse. It's not bad enough that this electronic brain assumes you are a thief; what it's really doing is rubbing it in about what a puny amount it is.

I have never received a big check from one of these machines, but my guess is that on a check for, let's say, $2,000, it prints "Only" instead of "Exactly." This is to convey the idea that, while $2,000 may be a lot to you, it isn't enough to keep an electronic brain supplied with ticker tape.

It's bad enough having the machines take over everything without their getting supercilious about it.

Maybe, when we pay our bills, we should put "Merely" in front of the amount to show that we've got lots more money where this came from. Or, instead of "Exactly," we could write "Approximately," which would indicate that money wasn't the sort of thing we thought important enough to worry about.

As I say, I'm not sure about the legal angles on all this, but what I would strive for would be to load the check with so much cuteness and whimsey that the payee would be too embarrassed to cash it.

Admittedly, American industry has sold a lot of breakfast food on the theory that it would make us strong and healthy. But this is in defiance of our basic American preference for things that we're told we shouldn't have. Take cholesterol, for example. We never heard of it until the doctors reported that it was slow poison. Now we insist on having a helping with every meal.

Think what the cereal people might have sold if they had said their product would make us feeble but devil-may-care.

Norman would boast to Elise, "I had three bowls of Nunkies this morning for breakfast. Hand shaking like a leaf. There's no tomorrow."

"Oh, no! You didn't really!" Elise would say, eyes aglow. "You will ruin your life. You need the love of a good woman."

¶ Of the two classic certainties, death and taxes, death is preferable. At least you're not called in six months later for an audit.

Dial your way to mental health

The clipping, as usual, is in my other suit, but it was about a motel that has a special room where guests may go and smash bottles, plates and glasses—hurl them right against a wall—to work off their frustrations.

I am not quite sure what this frustration consists of, or why it should be worse right now. The argument, I suppose, runs this way: Our society has increasingly deprived us of acceptable ways to express the urge for violence which lurks beneath our civilized exteriors. We cannot, as could the caveman, bash a neighbor or drag our wife around by the hair when we feel a vague unease.

Or, if we do these things, we find that we are in trouble with the law. Ramming other people's automobiles with our own is frowned upon, and even jumping up and down and screaming is considered Good Form only on certain specified occasions, such as athletic contests.

But what interests me is why anyone thinks it is necessary to go to such elaborate extremes as establishing a china-smashing room at a motel so we can purge ourselves of our hostilities.

Opportunities abound all around us. When it comes to facilities for defrustrating ourselves we are, I should think, far ahead of any other era of history.

I myself am, to stretch the definition a bit, a modern man. From time to time I spring from my chair and cry aloud, "I am suffering from the frustrations induced by our complex society."

No one in my intimate circle gets overheated about it. They do not rush me to a motel to break dishes. They know that therapy is close at hand. As close, to use the popular phrase, as your telephone.

I seize the phone and dial a number. A vibrant masculine voice tells me that the Ultimate National Bank will be glad to handle my estate.

"Why, you sneak," I shout into the mouthpiece, "I wouldn't trust you to stamp my parking ticket. I worked hard for that estate, buddy boy, and I'm not about to turn it over to a bunch of fat bankers with big cigars."

Now a sultry feminine voice comes on and says, "The ti-yum is ni-yun thuhurty thuree."

"O.K., buster," I say, "who's the dame you got in your office? You think I'm going to turn my overdraft, much less my estate, over to a bank that permits that kind of hanky-panky at 9:33 in the morning, you're crazy. Great Scott, man, the bank's only been open three minutes.

"And as for you, young lady, according to my watch I have here that I got from my great-uncle the railroad man, you are two minutes fast. That is, if what you really said was 9:33. It might have been 9:23. I don't know where you kids these days get that sloppy diction like you got there."

The man's voice comes back on to mention about my estate again and that gives me a chance to score him off for harping on the subject like some kind of ghoul or other.

There is another number I call which tells me when various airline flights will arrive and depart. With this one I work off my frustrations with the assistance of biting sarcasm.

If the voice intones, "Flight 682 from New York will arrive on time at 11:50," I will say, "I bet" or "Oh yeah?" or maybe just snort.

Sometimes I will dial an obviously impossible number just so I can tell the voice that chides me that we had the first telephone back in the old home town and that I was using a telephone before she was born and who does she think she is anyway? She replies that she is a recording and I tell her, "That's what you all say. It's just an excuse. That's the trouble with the world today. Instead of facing up to criticism, people just shrug their shoulders and say, 'What can I do about it, I'm just a recording.' "

Friends say that I am wasting my time talking back to these tapes, that nobody hears what I say. And that, of course, is the point. If there is anything I am, it's polite to real, live bankers, airline clerks and telephone operators. But with the recordings I work off the frustrations and nobody gets hurt.

And it's nowhere near as nutty—or messy—as smashing dishes.

An Air Force study of fairly recent vintage looked into the question of whether machines dream. Of course, they do. Or anyway the teletype does. I mention the teletype because it is the machine with which I have the closest professional contact.

In the main the teletype is a happy dreamer. As a reaction, I suppose, to the violence and urgency of the news it clicks out during its waking hours, it turns to a dream of bucolic innocence.

"The quick brown fox jumped over the lazy dog's back" is the burden of its recurrent dream.

Gone are Castro and Madame Nhu, Khrushchev and outer space. Instead the small, red figure of the fox, dainty in its quickness, leaps in a lovely arc over the old dog, sprawled upon the sun-dappled grass of a mountain meadow.

It pleases me to watch the teletype as it dreams of that magical tableau, where the quick fox never tires and the lazy dog lies in ecstatic somnolence, only occasionally lifting an eye to watch the orbit of the furry jumper etched against the blue sky of an eternal summer.

When I pass a dreaming teletype I walk softly. And I feel a twinge of sympathy when it rouses itself, mumbles a "TRFGHIJKL" and emits its first "BULLETIN . . . BULLETIN" of the day.

¶ The way things are going, the lightning will flash, the clouds will part and a Mighty Voice will announce, "This is the end of the world. This is the end of the world. This is a recording."

Did Edison feel like a filament?

The *Wall Street Journal* kindly calls my attention to a technique being used by large corporations to develop creative thinking among their employees. The point is to apply personal analogy to the problem.

Examples cited are a creative thinker who was able to think creatively about the matter of termite control by imagining himself to be a termite and of another who thought of himself as a carburetor in order to build a better one.

Well, *Wall Street Journal*, and creative thinkers everywhere, a lot of us have been using this technique for years.

I have a friend who is widely hailed for making the best martinis in town. When asked how he does it, he explains:

"I imagine that I am 3 ounces of gin. Then I ask myself how much vermouth I would like to have poured over me. I imagine how it would feel to be 3 ounces of gin and have 2 ounces of vermouth suddenly deluged down my neck. It would feel terrible. And so I work down until I (or rather not I-the-person but I-the-gin) hit upon the amount of vermouth that feels right. The trouble with most martinis is that they are not made from the gin's point of view."

A rather specialized case, I'll admit.

There are homelier illustrations. A few years back we planted some rather expensive seeds in our back yard. Nothing came up. My wife demanded to know what I intended to do about it, and I said I would investigate.

An hour later she found me curled up in a lounge chair and accused me of slacking the issue.

"Not at all," I replied. "I am imagining myself to be one of those seeds. I am interrogating myself as to whether I am getting enough water, or enough humus, or too much sun."

"What answer are you giving yourself?" she asked.

"The answer that keeps coming to mind," I said, "is that I am not getting enough sleep. The longer I lie here and try to interpret the situation as a seed would see it, the more I understand that rest is the most important ingredient. Rest sleep, peace. . . ."

It turned out my wife wanted the seeds grown by what it said on the package. But it is well known that the seeds don't write the package copy. I followed her advice and there were a few straggly blooms—nothing as compared to what I could have produced if I had been allowed a little more time to establish rapport with the seeds.

A neighbor lady who is married to a creative thinker reports that she came down one morning to find him regarding the coffee percolator.

"Where is the coffee?" asked the neighbor lady who is a career woman and has no time for stuff like making coffee.

"I am a percolator," her husband replied, creatively.

"Then why aren't you making coffee?" she asked.

"I don't know," he said. "That is what I am trying to find out."

"Do you feel plugged in?" she inquired.

"Yes."

"Do you contain four cups of water?"

He gurgled, just as the real percolator was doing.

"Then how come no coffee?"

"I don't know," he said miserably. Then he added, "Just a minute. I feel like I don't have any coffee grounds in my head."

Sure enough, that was the trouble.

"You see what creative thinking does?" his wife says proudly. "He would never have found out there were no coffee grounds in the percolator just by looking. He had to feel it subjectively."

Husbands are advised, however, to be selective in this field. When the kitchen faucet is leaking, it would not be a good idea to announce to the family that you will fix it as soon as you are able to imagine how it would feel to be a drip.

¶ The internal revenue service gives every American a number. Maybe the two great political parties could be realigned as the Odds and the Evens.

As you will recall, the electrical system in the Faith 7 went out, and Gordon Cooper had to land, or splash, the capsule himself. In a split second it was back to the days of the hand-cranked phonograph and the straight razor. The astronaut was equal to the challenge, and I wouldn't be surprised if he may have sparked a wave of enthusiasm to bring back people.

You could hear it in the voices on television, the amazed pride that the machines had chickened out and the whole project was being brought sweetly in by a human being. And this reaction was from men who spend their lives surrounded by computers and things that go whir and click and blip and are always popping up little numbers like the cash register in the supermarket.

I have had the feeling that Walter Cronkite hates these machines that are always blatting out the news that the Vermont gubernatorial race is settled before he feels we really need to know it. There is something demeaning to the human spirit, it seems to me, about a job which requires you to be constantly plugged into a socket.

If it's worth doing, it's worth deducting

Suppose you are an average American citizen—like the guy next door. Basically, your income is derived from a muck bean plantation, but you are also employed as a part-time race handicapper. Your youngest child is over 72 and going to college. The fourth floor of your house, which has been severely damaged by a falling meteorite, is rented out to the government for the use of Mohole scientists as a training camp.

The manager of the local baseball team is dependent upon you as his sole support. One of your oil wells has started pumping orange juice. Your great-aunt, a veteran of the First World War, has left the bulk of her fortune to your cat, which has only three legs.

Well, congratulations there, friend.

You are the one that the advice about How to Save Money on Your Income Tax is written for.

Especially if a great deal of your back pay has been impounded because you were held for a while in a Russian prison on an espionage charge and your gifts of art works to a nonprofit institution exceeded 17 per cent of your gross income.

If, of course, you are depending upon the birds to thin out your surplus cherry crop next summer, you will be interested in the deductions you can claim—the earlier the better—on the crumbs you put out for your feathered co-workers during the winter.

If you are claiming a Stutz Bearcat as an antique, while all the time you are using it as a business car, several interesting points of tax law arise.

The heartening thing is that pamphlets from the drugstore racks, columns in the daily press, half-hour interviews on the teevy answer all these questions, to say nothing of hundreds of others which closely affect the ordinary, run-of-the-mill tax-payer.

If a seven-ton monster of the horrendous deep is washed ashore in front of your beach house, can you claim it as a deduction due to the fact that its odor kept the mailman from delivering the news that you had won the Irish sweepstakes? Must you declare as income the money you received from selling balloons and little plastic souvenir monsters? If so, is this a capital gain, and may it be prorated over the approximately 350 years which is believed to be the life span of horrendous-deep-type monsters?

We ordinary people are, of course, appreciative of this advice. We don't know how we would get along without it.

But I can't help wondering if something couldn't be done for folks who don't fit the pattern. After all, the oddball, the man who might have special problems, pays taxes, too.

Just for example, to let our imaginations run completely wild, suppose you had a man who worked for a salary and had a home and a wife and a couple of children and a year-old car and didn't own any polo ponies or spend half the year in Puerto Rico.

I will concede that a man like this has to be a figment of our imagination. He doesn't exist.

But, merely as an exercise in ingenuity, would one of the tax experts suggest some way he could keep from going either (a) broke, or (b) to Leavenworth?

It would be, I humbly submit, entertaining. I realize, of course, that it would be diverting the tax expert from more pressing matters of interest to a wider audience, such as whether a professional shot-putter, who practices in his apartment, can deduct damage to the ceiling plaster of the people downstairs as a legitimate business expense.

¶ Some things are better than money. Such as, for example, inheriting the old family tax loophole.

Psst! a copy of Tropic of Corporation?

It will come as a surprise to no one who owns a share of stock that the annual reports of our corporations are no longer mere stuffy statistics. Instead they glow with four-color photographs, and pretty girls peer from between the refundable deposits and the accrued taxes.

Naturally this is a considerable advance, and the producer of the liveliest report gets an award and carries the title of vice-president in charge of stockholder relations or some such.

But have we gone quite far enough? Attractive though these brochures may be, can they compete with other reading matter?

They are admittedly seductive. If a company makes a little acetate thread, why, it emphasizes the fact with a picture of a lady going swimming. If it runs its power lines through open country, it shows lovely scenes of the countryside, demonstrating that the trees past which the power lines run in the spring are a different color than the ones they run past in the fall. It may not seem important for the stockholder to know this, but if it leads him on into the world of sinking-fund debentures and other delights, it is undoubtedly worth while.

Communication is what we are after here. We want the stockholder to understand what the company is up to. And I'm afraid we still aren't quite getting the message across.

What I would suggest is getting a little more of the impact of the paperback into these financial accounts. We could splash something like this across the cover:

"Torn from our files! The report they said couldn't be made! Now, in all its audacious fiduciary realism, the story behind Adulterated Fishhook, Inc."

Doesn't this, somehow, grab you a little more firmly than even the slickest of the new wave of reports, which seem to feel they are pretty far out if the headline is "Service Through Progress" or, as it sometimes is phrased, "Progress Through Service"?

There is a tremendous battle going on for the attention of the modern consumer. How about an approach like this one?

"Never before so frank, so daring an interim report. Dan Decimal, ace accountant, now for the first time reveals the naked truth about the undercover hi-jinks in the cashiers' department of Consolidated Misnomers & Son. 'Brutal'—*Wall Street News.* 'Corking yarn'—*Chicago Journal of Industry.*"

Or:

"Searing in its compassion! Only once a year does a report like this one come along. Compellingly stark! Starkly compelling! The story of the men of Nevermind Products (and the women!!!) and the money lust which drove them to service through progress."

Naturally we would need a lot of gaudy artwork. Maybe there could be a blonde, with the screaming words: "Long-term capital gain or refunded depreciation? Which? He had to know. You, too, will be spellbound by this hard-hitting story of a company's struggle against its conscience. We dare you to put it down. 'Holds reader's 4.3 per cent interest to the very end'— *Financial Digest.*"

Surely this is the logical next step in financial reports, and I can see only one drawback. The stockholder's wife won't let him bring it into the house.

¶ In an office with an efficient filing system, things are lost alphabetically.

Economics, a shirt-sleeve science

Always we must depend upon our creative personnel, the dreamers, seers and followers of the gleam to pull us out of the economic morass. But it seems unfair that the responsibility should fall upon the idea men of one particular industry year after year.

We all remember 1960, when the nation was flirting perilously with the doldrums. Leaders of great businesses realized that what was needed was a dynamic new thrust to start the ball rolling again.

But could Big Steel think of a new way to make steel?

No.

Similar failures of imaginative conceptualization occurred in motors, coal and gas.

Then suddenly, dramatically, the sports shirt industry snipped a little notch in the short sleeves of men's sports shirts. Who needs to be reminded how smokestacks once again started smoking, slowly assembly lines remeshed their gears, and giant corporations canceled their edicts for a rollback on expense-account lunches?

The little slit in the sports shirt sleeve was the ideal impetus for renewed confidence in the future of the nation. It served no useful purpose, but it immediately outmoded every existing sports shirt.

When, in 1962, the stock market once again put on a nervous performance, I instructed my wife to place our entire resources at the disposal of the economy.

Which she did, by buying me a sports shirt.

The moment I put it on, I realized that the creative brains of the sports shirt business had once again thrown themselves into the breach.

The sports shirt sleeves not only have the familiar notch in them, but at the top of the notch there is a—get this now—there is a button! Can you grasp the sheer, sweeping audacity of this move?

Can we visualize the meeting of the sports shirt tycoons? There are the usual fainthearted conservatives who want to retrench.

"How about," says one of them, a great name in sports shirt circles in years past—it was he who invented the transparent polo shirt so that you could always tell what kind of cigarette a man smoked because you could see through the pocket— "how about, in the face of the deteriorating economic situation, knocking off the button on the back of the collar?"

Well, the old man's opinions still inspire some respect, so the others are smoking their cigars and feeling the buttons on the backs of their collars and saying, "Sound thinking, J.P."

Then this young guy stands up, the Boy Wonder of Sports Shirts, and he says, "Now just a minute, fellows. We've heard a lot here about retrenching and cutting down and lopping off buttons. I say to you that this is not the spirit that built America.

"Suppose we knock off the button in the back of the collar, the way our revered friend, J.P., says. O.K., so men across the nation, maybe even in high places or our friends overseas, they notice that the button is gone from the back of the sports shirt collar. They start saying among themselves and putting it in diplomatic pouches that the sports shirt industry knows something—it's cutting down. First thing you know, we have a first-class hysterical panic on our hands.

"What I want to suggest to you is a breathtaking move—take the button off the collar, if you want—but add, repeat, add two more buttons."

Cries of "Where will we put them?" arise from the crowd.

"On the sleeves" is the triumphant reply. "One on each sleeve, just above the notch which, may I modestly remind you, was introduced by my revered Uncle Ed in time to save the country once before."

The market, of course, bounced back immediately. Ask not why there are little notches in sports shirt sleeves, nor why there are buttons above the notches; just be thankful that American industry has men who can dream.

The aim of every ambitious young American is to be a consultant. No profession has expanded and gained prestige so rapidly. The trouble is that we may be in danger of running out of new fields to consult in.

Even a few brief years ago this was all open range. If a man who yearned to consult found one area getting overcrowded, he merely pushed on toward the sunset. Were there too many child consultants? If so, it was no cause for discouragement; instead of consulting people about their children he could re-letter his sign and consult the same people about their marriage. Or their dining room draperies.

But gradually, just as the West was settled, all the available consulting areas seem to have been claimed. There are bridal consultants, management consultants, labor consultants, labor-management consultants, management-labor consultants, race-track consultants, gardening consultants, traffic consultants, diet consultants, expectant father consultants, and senior citizen consultants, to name only a few.

If you do not believe that the consultant explosion has the profession in a quandary, observe the number of practitioners who merely list themselves on their letterheads as "consultants" without stipulating any specialty.

I assume that, for the client who feels a need to consult but doesn't know what about, the general consultant has a list of categories on a big board behind his desk and the consultee can pick the one he wants.

Can a nation survive without adjectives?

The year 1968 will be remembered in history for the great strike in the public relations industry. At first few people realized the import when, early on the morning of June 5, Jack L. Flack, president of the Image Molders Union International (AFL-CIO) emerged from a hastily summoned last-ditch White House parley to announce grimly, "We're hitting the bricks."

Even well-informed sources thought that the work stoppage would have a minor effect on the lives of average Americans as compared with a shutdown in steel or rails.

But as typewriters clacked to a halt across the land and mimeograph machines gathered dust, the full impact began to be felt.

Parents of shapely young ladies wrote angry letters of protest to the newspapers. Nobody was coming around to measure their daughters and photograph them with a ribbon across their chest reading Miss Gum Spirits of Turpentine of 1968.

"Is this America," wrote Name Withheld of Quincy, Massachusetts, "where a man sacrifices himself so that his girl can be a lovely 36-24-36 and nobody cares, all on account of the power-mad greed of a handful of willful labor leaders?"

Charts of the royal succession of many an ancient title, Miss Fertilizer Spreader, Miss Sugar Beet, Miss Home Canning, bear merely a sad asterisk after the year 1968 to indicate that the contest was called because of the press agent strike.

Movie stars pouted petulantly and put up with their same spouses week after weary week as the strike dragged on, realizing that there really wasn't much point in changing mates if there was no press agent to write the real, inside heart-tugging story which would hit the cover of every fan magazine.

National Sack Lunch Week was canceled.

In Chicago, a 19-year-old boy who couldn't sing a note made a recording and immediately went back to work in the family grocery store, since there was no one to spread the word **among** the nation's teens that he was their new idol.

Irritating as these inconveniences were to the general **public,** they faded into insignificance as compared with the effect **the** strike had upon the national political conventions and the sub-sequent election campaign.

The kennel business was hard hit as candidates canceled their orders for photogenic dogs.

At least one leading prospect went fishing in deepest **secrecy,** trying to avoid the press.

Before the strike his public relations counsel had prepared **a** statement for him to use when the cameramen discovered him fishing: "A man should be left alone when he is fishing **or** praying. I will not tolerate this invasion of my privacy."

But because of the strike no cameramen showed up **and** he had to waste the entire day doing nothing but fishing, **a** sport he detested.

The conventions and the elections were, as you may re-member, a disaster. Candidates and keynoters and nomina-tors and introductory speakers were reading stuff they **had** pecked out all by themselves.

Caught without expert professional help, even veteran politi-cians were saying what they thought instead of what the public-ity staff thought that they should think.

It was a terrible time for the voters, faced with the problem of voting for men instead of images. No voter who experienced it would ever want to go through it again.

When the strike was finally settled, the nation heaved a **sigh** of relief as readers picked up their papers and saw that **a** prominent stage star's jewelry had been stolen and a Mid-western Senator had made a speech which, all the editorial writers agreed, would go down among the great oratorical **ex-**pressions of the human heart.

¶ On the list of Ten Best Anybodies, the **person you** never heard of is obviously the one who hired the **press agent** that got up the list.

¶ An elderly acquaintance says he has to keep on working. He spent all the money he was going to retire on to finance the hobby he was going to retire to.

The folksy bank bakes its own bread

I noticed that this old pal was looking rather haggard and unslept, and when I asked him about it he said it was because of the lumps in his mattress caused by the money he keeps there.

"Well," I said, "why don't you take your money to the bank? Are you old-fashionedly suspicious?"

"No," he replied. "I am shy."

"Shy?"

"Shy," he said. "And insecure. I don't know whether I could live up to the demands of the modern banking relationship."

I asked him what he meant and he spoke along these lines:

"They're so friendly. I read and see and hear the ads, and all the banks are sitting there waiting to take me by the hand, put an arm around my shoulder and really understand my problems. I ask myself why they would do this. They must want me to love them in return. I love banks in the sense that I love filling stations or post offices or hardware stores. I mean I have nothing against them. Live and let live is my motto and we are all put here to get along with one another according to the inscrutable plan.

"But life today is a continuous emotional drain. A man works hard all day, he loves his wife and his children and his cousins as far as the second remove. He is faced every day with a new nation or oppressed section of an old one that he must sympathize with.

"So he gets in the habit of crossing the street when he walks by a bank. I mean I know that my money would be safer there than in the mattress, but I just don't want to get emotionally involved.

"They keep telling me that they want to give me a free

ballpoint pen, or a silver service or if not a bicycle for my child, at least a balloon. It's embarrassing. You sort of feel that if you go into a bank they'll be warmhearted and friendly, but won't they really be wondering whether you are there out of reciprocal warmth and friendship or because you want a ballpoint pen?

"I have these nightmares, which is why I cross the street away from the bank, that they are sending vice-presidents out to drag me in off the sidewalk and force money on me.

"Maybe this is silly of me. But I feel that friendship is a two-way street, know what I mean? I just wouldn't be comfortable, taking all these things from the bank and not giving anything."

"You could give the president a ballpoint pen," I said. "Or a balloon."

"I tried that," he said. "It was the last time I opened a savings account and I got a cigar and an orchid to take home to my wife. Well, the next day I took a jar of jelly by the bank for the president, and his secretary said she would give it to him. I thought she was kind of chilly and asked her if she wasn't interested, like their advertising said, in my personal problem. 'You really have one, don't you?' was her answer.

"So I took my money out of that bank, and it's all in the mattress."

"You thought they were not properly appreciative of the jelly?" I asked.

"No," he went on, "I knew that these were kindly folks. Remember when bankers were bankers? Not any more. Now they are folks. And I got to thinking that when that girl gave the president the jelly he would have his wife call up my wife and invite us over for dinner, and then we'd have to have them back, and he could deduct it because I was a customer, but I couldn't afford to have this banker and his wife over for dinner out of my own pocket every other week or so.

"And I know enough about the new image of banking that he would be looking at me reproachfully every time we met and wanting to know why I hadn't dropped by in the last few days to pick up some more money. It's kind of uncomfortable sleeping on that cash, I'll admit. But it beats lying awake thinking about some friendly, folksy, kindly banker I had accepted a ballpoint pen from and then not even given him the courtesy of letting him lend me any money.

"I used to get along just wonderful with bankers when they were flinty-hearted and cold-eyed and throwing orphans out in the snow. But now I don't dare go near them. They are too nice."

We parted company, he back to stuff some more money in his mattress and I to my bank to pick up some free matches and weigh myself on the scale in the lobby.

When you meet anyone from another town or city, it is important to let him know that you are familiar with the place, even if you aren't. This establishes an immediate bond between you, and he will be amenable to the purchase of whatever it is you want him to buy, be it insurance policy, automobile or the next round of drinks.

Bennett Cerf on the teevy is very good at this. If someone on the quiz show says he is from Moscow, Idaho, Bennett will say, "Do you have any connection with the famous University of Idaho, which is located there?"

Whether there is any connection or not, the fellow will naturally have a warm feeling for Bennett and maybe, when the rest of the panel isn't looking, will make little wiggly motions with his fingers, tipping him off that his line is rearing angleworms.

¶ Automation won't be complete until every machine that dispenses cigarettes has one right next to it which bums them back.

Do we need an image subsidy?

Secretary Orville Freeman of the Agriculture Department convoked a blurb of public relations counselors to see what could be done about the image being projected by the farmer.

"It's bad enough I got to milk the cows," said a farming friend, "do the ploughing, keep up the paper work and fix the transmission on the jeep. Now I got to project an image, too?"

According to the Secretary, the farming friend needs an image that will arouse the public which is treating the farmer with apathy.

People, according to the Secretary, are even antagonistic toward the farmer.

I don't know where the Secretary gets his facts, but I assume they are accurate like all the other information the government gets. I suppose a survey has been run and people have said, "I can take farmers or leave them alone" (apathy) or "I hate farmers" (antagonism).

But I have never run into anybody who felt that way. Most of us who live in cities are almost abjectly grateful to the farmer. We explain to our children that if it weren't for the farmer there would be no teevy dinners, and we tell them that milk doesn't come in bottles or cartons but in cows. And we say, "If you do not eat your spinach you will hurt the farmer's feelings."

Still, I will go along with the Secretary. If he says the farmers need an image, then I'll believe him.

After all, the Secretary of Defense has developed an image for our soldiers; the Secretary of Labor has an image for labor. It must be rather embarrassing for the Secretary of Agriculture to be the only Cabinet member who hasn't got an image for his constituency.

The question is: What image should the farmer project?

And here is where, I am afraid, we may have some trouble. I think Mr. Freeman is going to need more than the four public relations experts he has summoned to assist him.

They're going to have to decide exactly what agriculture is—a science, an industry, a way of life, a political bloc or a state of mind. Is the farmer a soil chemist, a businessman, a part-time factory worker or a rural philosopher?

It's not going to be easy choosing one image. When the farmer projected a clear-cut image of somebody named Si or Hiram, wearing chin whiskers, bib overalls and high-top boots, he was a universal favorite.

But I don't think the public relations geniuses are going to revive the image of Hiram. Nor would the farmers (and especially the farmers' wives and daughters) hold still for it.

So there will be some uneasy weeks ahead on the farm, as the folks wait to find out just what their image is to be. Once it is established, of course, it will fit easily into the traditional patterns of rural conversation with such mild pleasantries as "Do you think the rain will hurt the images?"

And let us have no ill-informed comment about paying the farmer not to project.

I am convinced that there is a segment of the farm population which checks through the available printed matter looking for the word "farmer." Then this segment takes up its pen to suggest that if so-called city peaheads would leave the farmer alone, the nation would be a lot better off.

Farmers and farmers' wives lost no time in pointing out that they (or their husbands) work harder than I do, that they get up earlier and deserve a larger slice of the national pie for their efforts. The fact that I more or less agree with them doesn't mean that I can see any connection between these propositions and my discussion of the farmer's image.

Apparently it makes little difference what the article says. The presence of the word "farmer" is enough to convince this segment (and this segment's wife) that something unpleasant is being said.

"Teen-ager" is another trigger word. Just write it and you hear from every student council within indignation range, asking how come you don't write about the 97.8 per cent of today's fine Junior Citizens who have never beaten up an elderly shopkeeper in all their brief but immaculate lives, and reminding you that your own generation toted hip flasks, dumped all that tea in Boston Harbor and sang "The Hut Sut Song."

Not that the farmers and the teen-agers are the only ones who have developed image sensitivity. Without regard to race, creed, occupation or age, people are hiring public relations counsel to sandpaper their nerve ends. They just know that somebody is bad-mouthing them and they can't rest easy until they know who it is and what they are saying.

This makes it awfully tough on us laymen—meaning, I guess, those of us with no particular race, creed, occupation or age. The Missouri Bar Association dealt us a severe blow when it sponsored a survey which revealed that lawyers have the feeling that people don't like them.

This came fast on the heels of an announcement by the president of the American Medical Association that doctors have a bad image.

I'm just not sure that we laymen, broad though our shoulders are, can take on both these accounts at once. And this is without considering the other professions which are lining up at the microphone to report that nobody is being nice enough to them, either.

It used to be you could go to the doctor and say, "Sam, I got this ringing feeling sort of in my right ear and a pain in my left shoulder bone, and what are you going to do about it?"

He would say there was a lot of it going around or that you had to expect this sort of thing at your age or tell you to quit eating hot biscuits for breakfast or have all your teeth pulled out or write you out a prescription for some green and yellow pills.

And that was it.

Nowadays, before you get past the first symptom, he says, "Why do you hate doctors?"

"I don't, Sam," you say. "I like doctors. Some of my best friends—"

"You do hate doctors," he will snap. "It's in the survey. You don't like my image."

"I didn't even know you had one, Sam. Now, about this ringing—"

"Never mind that," he will continue. "You think I make too much money. It's all in the survey."

"Sam," you will say, "I don't know anything about your money; all I know is that there is this ringing, or more of a buzzing—"

He will look at you with those big, reproachful eyes and say, "You think I treat you like a number. That I am cold and impersonal, not like the old family doctor."

"Sam, believe me," you will have to assure him, "never like a number. You never treated me that way. You've always been extremely warm and personal with me, Sam. Sometimes I wish you weren't so personal. I like you better than the old family doctor. I will call you 'Doc' if it will make you feel better. Now about this shoulder bone—"

"You want to socialize me because you don't think I make night calls," he will say.

"Sam," you will say, "I'll call you at 3 o'clock every morning and you can run right over."

"You think I play too much golf," he will go on, and about half the time you flee the scene before anything ever gets done about the ringing and the shoulder bone.

Now it is going to be the same way with the lawyer.

If you tell him, "Counselor, I got this bad rap from a neighbor on account of my child fell out of his apple tree onto his wife's best quilt that was hanging on the line, and I need a fast defense," he is going to be just like the doctor.

"You don't think you will get a fair trial, do you?" he will ask.

"Sure, sure," you will say. "I am a great believer in the courts and our system of jurisprudence, but how about the kid and the apple tree?"

"Forty per cent of you laity think my bills are too high," he will go on, waving his spectacles like he was in the courtroom. "It's all in the survey."

"Counselor," you will assure him, "I don't think you charge nearly enough. Charge anything. But let's get on the case before this quilt maniac gets me thrown in jail—"

"You have no faith in the jury system," he accuses. "It says so in the report."

"I love the jury system," you will insist. "Some of my best friends . . ."

But it will do no more good with the lawyer than with the doctor or the farmer or, in due course, with the engineer, contractor, plumber or almost any specialty. They are all financing surveys to show how punk their image is.

It's rough on us laymen. We have to spend so much time soothing the professionals and sending them flowers and bringing a smile to their wan faces that we have time for very little else.

Maybe what the laity needs to do is have a survey that shows that laymen have a bad image. Then, it might be, we could get some sympathy too.

¶ THE ONLY GOOD TREND
IS A SPOTTED TREND

If I were looking for an easier go I would be an anthropologist, especially a British one. All you do is hurtle off the jet at Kennedy International and immediately yell, "O.K., everybody, cut out the fertility rites."

Next morning you are on the front pages and all week you are appearing on radio or television programs where some lady is asking how you spell "puberty" and saying, kittenishly, for you to wait a minute because she has to perform an old folk ritual known as pushing the product. Or you are sitting around in a panel with everybody flicking angry ashes off their cigarettes or chewing on the earpieces of their spectacles. You are the one with the thoughtful pipe and the expression of gentle aloofness.

The picture magazines show you examining a warren of skull bones and giving your opinion that our college football games are reminiscent of the yak sacrifices of primitive Tibet. You will be put under contract by a publisher to analyze our national political conventions. You can write the book ahead of time, comparing the occasion to the way the tree-dwelling Auca Indians of Venezuela select their chief.

To get in on this dodge, however, you have to have a degree in fertility or, at the very least, puberty.

The best the untutored journalist can do is spot trends. Trend spotting is not nearly as scholarly as anthropology, but just about as useful.

"Leave no trend unspotted" is the motto of the observer of the contemporary scene.

Too many people think that trend spotting is easy. As a result they spot trends the way some hunters shoot deer, bagging the cow, a fellow hunter or the farmer's wife and television set.

The good trend spotter must, first of all, make sure that it *is* a trend before he spots it. Some of these trigger-happy trend spotters, the first time there is a slight rustle in the undergrowth of our civilization, they go, "Spot!" It may not be a trend at all, or if it is, it's only a little baby trend that never gets a chance to grow up on account of being spotted to death.

The real pro holds his spot until he is sure that the trend is a mature one and worth spotting; then he spots it, delicately, softly, so as not to frighten it away. Timing is all, because there is the obvious danger that if he waits too long other trend spotters will move in first and the trend will be overspotted before he gets to it.

I suppose that anthropology has its satisfactions, such as knowing that you were the first to compare back-yard cookery in America to the burnt sacrifices of the Druids, but I wonder if they are any more warming than those of the man who can exhibit a trend to admiring friends, smile modestly and say, "I spotted it myself."

If a disease is worth having it's worth supporting

¶ A friend, who is active in community affairs, faces the future calmly. No matter what disease he dies of, he's on the board.

¶ There are no standards any more. The new man on the FBI's Ten Most Wanted list isn't even tattooed, and the common cold is to have a foundation of its own.

Hang a hankie in the window; we'll be coming around with our Crusade Against Subcutaneous Hypochondria. It is the last of the major diseases to be left without a national foundation, and now at last this gap in our health bulwark is being plugged.

The Crusade Against Subcutaneous Hypochondria will be referred to in press releases as CASH, which is why we've got that word Subcutaneous in there. It doesn't mean anything, but it has a medical sound to it, and we need the S for cuteness.

Hypochondria is the ideal disease for foundation purposes. It afflicts 99.5 per cent of the population from the cradle to the grave. It can't be cured, so that almost no funds will have to be diverted to research. Instead, CASH pledges that all but a small dribble of the money you contribute will go toward salary, long lunches for the staff, public relations and maintaining a luxurious headquarters building.

Not that there won't be a certain irreducible minimum of research. A number of photogenic young people with college degrees or the equivalent will be employed to have their pictures taken for the foundation's weekly publication, *The CASH Register.*

They will wear white coats and pose with white mice.

There will be some white mice, never fear, as we will want to know whether hypochondria thrives best under a system of free medical care or socialized medicine.

Carefully controlled experiments will subject perfectly healthy mice to a barrage of television commercials, advertisements, political speeches and *Reader's Digest* articles to see how long it takes them to show signs of hypochondria.

Preliminary studies, it should be said, indicate that the average white mouse, placed on a diet of *Ben Casey* and the women's magazines is, within two months, convinced that it has every disease from aphasia to zymosis.

White mice, in the laboratory, are developing the symptoms of diseases that it is impossible for white mice to have. This, obviously, is pure-D hypochondria, and may be considered a major breakthrough.

Medical and other leaders who prefer to remain anonymous think that hypochondria is the coming disease. Every day we are absorbing through our ears, eyes and pores a tremendous fallout of information, rumors, propaganda and guesses about our physical condition. We awake to a radio announcer's discussion of the turmoil in our gastric regions. We lunch on the medical columnist's opinions about our cholesterol. We fall asleep with the weekly picture magazine's brain operation in living color.

From Washington we hear that we will suffer through long, unattended periods of senility if Medicare is not passed; and from the American Medical Association that if it is passed we will be cast afloat upon the stormy waters of political medication.

Absorbing this massive dosage is bound to raise our medical obsession well above the level of normal tolerance. Acute hypochondria will sweep the country like the plague.

We cannot afford to stall around until it is too late. If hypochondria is to be the disease of the future, it deserves a foundation with a highly paid honorary chairman. (A name or two suggest themselves.) Back CASH with Cash Today!

Even the conversation is catered

I am not telling you that the funny record is new. I remember "Cohen on the Telephone" and at one time could recite large chunks of "The Two Black Crows" with the precocity which the modern child shows in chanting beer commercials.

But we must admit that the trend is up in this item. Sales figures indicate that Americans are gathering in little clumps to hear the various *opera* of the Messrs. Berman, Newhart, Meader, Sherman, *et al.*

And so the phonograph steadily expands its boons to humanity. Its first service was to provide us with music, thus making it unnecessary for the family to sing or play upon the gay banjo. Now the recording industry is taking care of humor in the home.

Many a family has been riven by Father's jokes. More fledglings have departed the nest because they couldn't stand one more repetition of Dad's thigh-slappers than have been driven out by any other cause, including overdiscipline or a desire to dance in the *Follies*.

Harmony surely will reign in the household which is well stocked with comic record albums. No more of Dad's home-hewn corn when the rib-ticklers of the most elegant professional practitioners of funny are constantly on tap.

Moving beyond the family circle, we find that the funny record is a splendid saver of time and effort at social gatherings. Guest and host alike are freed from the responsibility of wit. Nobody any longer needs to memorize a joke before going out into company.

The records take care of the humor and you can merely limit yourself to desultory comment about the color of the draperies and how nice everybody looks.

But is humor all?

Why shouldn't the records take over the entire party? My proposed company, as soon as some financing details are worked out, will provide a complete conversational service for the Occasion of Your Choice.

The way I envision this, you go to the Whomevers' house, surrender your coat and hat and sit down. Winona Whomever puts on the new LP album, "Banality in Stereo." You sit there, sipping the Drink of Your Choice, puffing on the Weed of Your Choice, making eyes at the Girl of Your Choice, or merely staring at the Corner of the Ceiling of Your Choice.

From the phonograph comes all the appropriate talk: "Yes, well, I don't pretend to be an expert, but if it had been my quarterback I'd have passed on third down." . . . "I'm not sure what's in them but they are these big yellow and purple capsules that Mavis Camshaft says have made a new woman of her." . . . "But you have to look at it from the standpoint of the average Vietnamese." . . . "Of course, it's a growth stock and my broker said, 'Clarabelle, you're a regular riverboat gambler.' " . . .

"He wrote us last week that his grades weren't very good but he was gaining some meaningful insights." . . . "Understand, I'm not criticizing the administration's specific actions, it's just that I can't conceptualize the frame of reference." . . . "Thank you, Mona, it's really a very simple recipe, if you have mushroom soup and slivered almonds." . . . "I told him that I was working for the company before he was old enough to dodge the draft." . . .

There would be sound effects on the records, too—giggles and an occasional scream, the tinkle of glasses, the crash of a dropped tray.

With a really efficient, three-turntable system, you could put on the conversation record, a funny record and some background music and, as far as I can see, you could do away with guests entirely.

Think of the saving—just start the records, go upstairs, shut the bedroom door tightly and you are asleep by 10 o'clock with the neighbors none the wiser.

¶ Modern parents are tape-recording their children earlier and earlier. "Sorry, Doctor, I got some feedback on that first tape. Would you mind slapping the baby again?"

It's smart to live in the past if you sell souvenirs

Dear Doctor: I am addressing you as doctor because surely whatever else happens to civilization, the Ph.D. will survive. In fact, it may be that the Ph.D.s will take over the world, instead of the ants who, heretofore, have attracted most of the smart money.

Be that as it may, and even if you are only a graduate student working toward your doctorate, I respect you as I do all archaeologists. I should think that there would be nothing more fascinating than rummaging around in the ruck and rubble of the remains of a vanished race and trying to reconstruct what those old people were like and what in the world they thought they were doing anyway.

For example, you come up with a ring that you say is what

the court ladies of the Fan Tan dynasty wore in their noses, and your article is the smash hit of the June issue of the *Archaeological News*. Then some wise guy at Harvard says you are a fraud or at best a hoax perpetrator and that this is either a pawn used in a game by children during the pre-Columbian era or part of the door-latch mechanism of a 1926 Essex. As I say, fascinating.

What I want to get across, Doctor, is that I feel a real empathy for archaeologists, so anything that I can do to lighten the load is the least I can give in return for all the pleasure I have gotten out of reading various archaeological flashes and bulletins through the years.

Which is why I have written this letter and put it in this tin box where I keep all the important stuff like, well let's see, the guarantee for an electric mixer that wore out ten years ago, a recipe pamphlet from a company that makes rum which I hate, an insurance policy, the receipt for the license on a long-departed dog, and so on. It's hard to say how long this tin box will survive the ultimate end of things, but I'd say it has about the best chance of anything in the house.

One word about that, though. If, by one of those freaks of history, this house should be preserved as perfectly as, say, Pompeii, you may not ever find this letter. There are an awful lot of boxes in this house. Most of them are empty.

I'm not expecting everything to be wiped out, of course—not for a few centuries. But in case something should happen pretty soon, I want to explain about the boxes. In case you find this note. Which, considering all the boxes, you may not.

I am assuming that you are a dedicated archaeologist. A man just about has to be, doesn't he? I mean, to be in the business at all. Because I'm pretty sure that one thing won't have changed in the however many centuries it will have been between the time I write this and the time you read it. You scholars and teachers are still underpaid. Am I right?

The thing you are going to wonder about is why the average home in the United States of America (which is where what you are standing on used to be) had all these empty boxes. Doctor, many an average United States of America husband wonders the same thing.

If, as I say, you are dedicated (which, on account of the low pay, you are bound to be), you are going to start opening all these boxes. And you are going to find most of them empty. Especially if you are digging down from the top. This means you will hit the attic first. And that's all solid empty boxes. Worse than that, there are empty boxes within empty boxes within, etc.

Eventually, dedicated or no, you are going to get tired of opening boxes and finding nothing inside except nothing—or maybe another empty box. So you may give up and not ever open this box and miss the note, which would be an archaeological pity.

Because you will write a monograph about the significance of empty-box worship in our civilization and you have several chances of being wrong. You may think that these empty boxes represent our ancestors, or are a form of currency.

But the plain fact is that the average house has all these empty boxes because the average wife thinks that someday she will need them to put things in. She never does, and this, as you can see, is why the boxes pile up.

Well, what I started out to warn you about was that a big fad right now is reconstructing colonial villages and old country stores and forts and castles and riverboats and who knows what all, and I can see how they are going to mess you up if you get these tourist attractions confused with the real thing.

I mean, what are you going to make of a log blockhouse with a TV aerial on the roof, or a Wild West frontier town with a parking lot?

But I'll have to write you another note about that. I got off, as you see, on this empty-box thing, and already this letter is pretty long, considering that the language will probably be obsolete when you find this (if you do) and it's going to be one heck of a job deciphering it. I hope you think it was worth it.

CHRISTIAN COLLEGE LIBRARY
COLUMBIA, MISSOURI

¶ A move to attract the tourist dollar by restoring the Old Home Town to the way it looked in 1890 fell through when Alderman Adkins pointed out that it still looks that way.

Eventually beauty contests are going to have to include girls from other planets, and we will be reading stories like this:

"The new Miss Galaxie, a smiling, vivacious milligram of algae, Miss Krk-3 Np, representing the planet Mercury, was crowned last night.

"She said it was the happiest night of her entire 3 million years and that she has two sisters at home who are prettier than she is. Her measurements are .0036, .0024, .0036 milligrams.

"Miss Krk-3 Np is the first entrant from a planet other than Earth to win the title. Her triumph came after the contest had been rocked by charges that she was not a girl but a vegetable. Miss Norway resigned from the competition, saying that she was not going to be maid in waiting to a fungus.

"Most of the other Earth beauties, however, reported that they got along well with the girls from other planets, and Miss Venus, a striking eight-armed, two-ton light-bluish blonde, was voted Miss Congeniality."

Who's that out there serenading my aspidistra?

¶ Either heaven or hell will have continuous background music. Which one you think it will be tells a lot about you.

There may be no really good day for discussing the plot of corn at Normal, Illinois, which has music played to it. But if discuss it we must, let's get on with it.

George E. Smith, the man who serenades the corn, reports that the yield was 137.5 bushels per acre, whereas corn which was grown under identical conditions, but with music omitted, produced only 116.8 bushels.

It's what we have been trying to sell for years—the idea that people, plants, anything that lives, have to know that somebody cares.

People who think that standing in a lonely corn plot in the middle of Illinois and growing without the encouragement of the music of the masters—if it's only Verdi or, for that matter, Cole Porter or, for that matter, Chubby Checker—is easy are people who have never tried it. You take an ear of corn that has had a gypsy violin played at it, and you have an ear of corn that is tender, yielding, atremble with an urge for succulence. Having received so much pleasure, it naturally wants to give some in return. This is Nature's law, and those who mess around with it end up with hard, flavorless corn, unloved and unloving.

I don't know what Mr. Smith's theory of playing music in the cornfield may be. He may have something scientific in mind, something to do with sonic vibrations and that sort of thing. I prefer to think that what is operating in Normal is deeper, closer to the mainspring of all life—i.e., romance.

I often whistle at my lawn. While the neighbors are fertilizing and seeding and raking and mulching, I am strolling around the acreage emitting choruses of "Let Me Call You Sweetheart." As a result I have grass. Most of it, true, is crabgrass. But this merely underlines the point. Crabgrass is so used to being badly used and the butt of television jokes that it responds ecstatically to the smallest sign of affection.

If the music is persisted in, the crabgrass will eventually take it more calmly and the bent Bermuda will get a chance to show how it can respond to melodic inspiration.

In the event that you are not a skilled *siffleur* and lack the electronic equipment for disseminating music around the premises, an occasional word of love or encouragement to your plant life may prove equally effective.

Don't treat your house plants as though they were part of the furniture. Tell them that they are members of the family, compliment them on their appearance, give them a "Nice going, there," whether or not they have earned it.

If this program works on corn and aspidistra, think how much more valuable it would be when applied to livelier species, such as wives. Give your wife Mantovani on the record player, slip her compliments, such as that she is a great little kid, and she will bloom like 137.5-bushel corn.

You will have a big, healthy wife whom you will be proud to show to the neighbors and take to the county fair.

Wives are just as important as corn, and don't let us forget it.

¶ It figures that music would be good for crops. We've all noticed that flowers bloom best in the spring on account of all the poetry that is spread around at that time of the year.

Nobody crushes Truth to earth around Washington, and hasn't for years. What has happened is that Truth is now managed with as great care and consideration as is any other natural resource. Obviously, a nation without Truth isn't going to get along any better than a nation without water, oil or wheat. So it has seemed an increasingly wise course over the years to ration out the supply of Truth, to make sure it doesn't suffer from disastrous depletion. Our descendants would never forgive us if we exhausted all the Truth and left none for them.

Which is why Washington's Birthday is always a time of peril in the city named after him. Carried away by the enthusiasm for the Truth which is associated with our country's most revered figure, thoughtless elements might call for the uncontrolled massive squandering of our Truth resources.

One can almost imagine a Federal government as prodigal of the Truth as of money, spending the Truth, throwing it out the windows and pouring it down rat holes as though it were going out of style.

Cooler heads invariably prevail. They realize that the truth policy of George Washington's simpler day is not feasible in the modern world. A conservative attitude toward Truth, it seems safe to say, will continue.

Will success spoil culture?

¶ A wise painter of abstractions will price his work at some figure such as $69 so that it won't lose value when exhibited upside down.

A thinker has asked me why sports are on the bum in America while painting, sculpture, poetry and chamber music are packing the houses.

With a trembling larynx he pointed out that a Picasso brings more on the open market than a major league shortstop and that the poet in residence at large universities makes more than the defensive backfield coach.

I explained to him what he should have been able to figure out for himself.

"It is," I said, "the cult of the obscure. This is what makes art so challenging today. To enjoy it you have to participate. You have to figure out what the painter, poet or whatever has in mind. You are there. It's a challenge.

"Sport, on the other hand, is cut-and-dried. It is played according to rules and with a record book and a grounds crew to come out every morning to re-ink the playing field. Ritual has killed more important things than sport.

"Look at the arts. There was a time when they nearly went the way of croquet because of too many conventions and traditions and this-is-the-way-to-do-its. You painted a hand like a hand and put tunes in your music and the poetry went a-b-a-b-c-c. Very dull. It drove the customers away, and who's to blame them for leaving?"

The thinker said he assumed that this had been changed.

"Of course," I said impatiently, "are you some sort of noddy not to have noticed that in the *beaux-arts* all is free-form, experimental, unhampered by rules or preconceptions?"

He said that he had, come to think of it, observed something of this sort.

"All right," I said, "and the people love it. When a man can spend a half hour in an art museum looking at a yellow dot on a solid black canvas, delving for the deeper meaning, why should he go out and waste his time watching a sport which is still played more or less the same way it was when he was a small boy?"

"I don't know," said the thinker, "but I suppose you have a solution?"

"Naturally," I replied. "Free-form sports. Think of the excitement, the tension, if you were told that for $4 you could buy a ticket to a game that the players would make up as they went along."

"Like basketball?" he asked.

"Flippancy," I said, "has no part."

"Sorry," he mumbled.

"People," I said, "pay much more than that to go to a show in New York where all they know when they leave is that it has been a rich experience. They haven't the slightest idea what it means. They are enraptured.

"What I envision is a stadium where 45,000 people gather. One team of players has eleven men, the other has six and there are several players who belong to neither team but are just sort of improvising. The referees have a rule book written in a language they can't understand.

"All afternoon the players throw, kick, dribble, swim, run, wrestle, dive and anything else that comes into their minds. At the end—or rather not at the end, because there is no end—the loudspeaker announces that the losing combatant has emerged victorious. Everybody goes home happy."

"And the fans would like it?" he asked.

"They'd be nuts about it," I said. "Look at sports today— somebody hits the ball farther or runs faster, or breaks this record or that. What's to talk about? With abstract sports they could argue all the way home and far into the night as to what was the inner significance."

"You may be right," he said.

"I doubt it," I responded.

They don't make monsters like King Kong any more

Thanks to the twin modern miracles of television and insomnia, I have been catching up with the late, late monster movies, and I have discovered a rather frightening thing about myself. I am always on the side of the monster.

I identify with the monster. Not that I particularly want to. Every time when something comes on, like *The Gigantic Toad*, let's say, I make up my mind I am going to be objective. I tell myself that there are two sides to every story and I am going to give the people a fair hearing, the same as I intend to give the monster.

But it doesn't work. I don't think like these people. I wouldn't mind, really, if the Gigantic Toad moved in next door, but I don't think I'd want the members of the expedition anywhere on the same block.

There is the leader, Professor Norm. I wouldn't trust him to lead me to the corner drugstore. He is always squinting into a microscope and shaking his head and saying, "There is something here I don't understand." All the time the Gigantic Toad is looking over his shoulder.

His daughter Ileona isn't much smarter and besides is a terrible runner. She is very knock-kneed and wears jodhpurs to accentuate the fact. She has to do a lot of running because the Gigantic Toad is always hopping after her. She slows down the whole expedition. They have to stop and help her over any rock more than six inches high.

That's another thing I have against Professor Norm. He should have left the kid home; she is a troublemaker.

Dr. Gorb, the handsome physicist, is in love with her and so is fat and ugly Dr. Zok, the biologist.

Then there are two enlisted men off the ship whom we really never get to know. They are put in there for the Gigantic Toad to eat early in the picture. Monsters always devour the expedition in reverse order of rank. I don't hold this against the monster. These people are the type who put the leaders in a Quonset hut and leave the enlisted men out in a pup tent where the Gigantic Toad can't help but stumble over them.

Put yourself in the Gigantic Toad's place. He has been lying there in the primordial ooze for a few thousand years, bothering nobody. If the world is full of wars and folk singing, smog and slums, traffic jams and atom bombs, they are none of his doing. Suddenly, who shows up but a bunch of nowhere actors thinly disguised as a scientific expedition, throwing C-ration cans in his lagoon and playing the radio until all hours.

You couldn't blame him for getting sore. As a matter of fact, he shows considerable restraint. He merely hops up on the atoll to ask these intruders to hold it down to a gentle roar. They panic and start shooting at him.

Then he sees Ileona Norm. He flips for her. Ileona may not be the greatest, but she's the only girl in the cast.

Another thing about nutty Ileona is that you would think after a few weeks on that island with nobody around but her father and Dr. Gorb and Dr. Zok, a Gigantic Toad would look good. But no, she has to scream and run away, and when the Gigantic Toad merely hops after her to try to explain things, there are more shots and radioed appeals for the Air Force to send over a B-186.

Who is going to criticize a man, or a Gigantic Toad, for admiring a girl (even if she is knock-kneed)? Through it all the Gigantic Toad behaves with perfect calm and dignity. It is the people who are yelling and falling down and waving their arms about.

This, I think, is why I identify with the monsters. They are what I would like to think of myself as—romantic, yet gentle; powerful, but peace-loving.

Most important of all, these monsters have high artistic standards. They just can't stand punk acting. They are patient, more patient than I would be. But after an hour or so of listening to the expedition mouth its lines and mug at the camera, the Gigantic Toad can't stand it any more. He eats up as much of the cast as he can get to.

And I am sitting there in front of the teevy, saying, "Attaboy, Gigantic, now go after Gorb—he's hiding over there behind that boulder with the dame."

But the monster always loses. The script is stacked against him. I haven't given up hope. The Indians are getting a better break in the Westerns, and maybe the pendulum will swing in favor of the Gigantic Toads, Blobs, Things and all the others I like to think of as My Team.

¶ The Indians are doing better on television, which is encouraging. Eventually we may see a show where the patients win out over the interns.

A man is known by the scapegoats he keeps

¶ Unusual weather is blamed on the atomic bomb, and it's a safe bet that the first bow and arrow took the rap for the unseasonableness of the following spring.

"Why is it, I wonder," she wanted to know, "that companies send out self-addressed envelopes that are just a fraction of an inch too small to put their own return statements in?"

"It's an international plot," her husband replied.

"Who is behind it?" she inquired.

"Oh," he answered, "the usual bunch—the Communists, the Fascists, the bankers, the mass media, the unions, the big corporations, Dean Rusk, the National Council of Churches, the Jews, the Pope, the American Medical Association, Edward R. Murrow, people who want to fluoridate the water, the oil interests, UNESCO, Hearst, the Mental Health Foundation, foreigners, Rockefeller, Ford, Norman Thomas, the NAACP, the NCAA, Harvard University, the Planned Parenthood Association, the Birch Society, Frank Costello, J. Edgar Hoover, Joe Kennedy, NBC, *The New York Times,* Norman Mailer, Henry Luce, Ford Frick, the Krupp family, Willi Brandt, de Gaulle, U Thant, real estate dealers, Newton Minow, Blue Cross, the Daughters of the American Revolution, the Americans for Democratic Action, Frank Sinatra, the National Geographical Society."

"The, in other words, rat pack?" she inquired.

"That's what I said," he agreed. "The usual bunch."

"What is their interest in this matter?"

"It makes no difference," he explained. "The whole point is that everything these days is an international plot—sometimes a national plot, but usually international."

"I feel sorry," she said, "for women who do not have wonderful husbands who go out into the marketplace and saloon and report back with word of what is really going on. If it had not been for you making it all crystal-clear, I would have thought this was merely a case of stupidity instead of a worldwide operation by a far-flung secret apparatus."

"Too true," he said. "A man these days has to put in full time at the, as you say, marketplace and saloon, to know who is really manipulating the world. If it were not for innate delicacy, I would pull out my shirttail and show you the black-and-blues I have received in the course of my research."

"You have been attacked by the hired agents of this supersecret apparatus before whom Presidents and Prime Ministers tremble? You have been followed home from your place of employment?" she gasped. "Haven't I always warned you, Sam, to always take the second taxicab?"

"You have," he said, "even though you know my allowance only permits the bus, which is another sign of how the hidden manipulators pull the strings which operate the Supreme Court, the armed services, the Congress and the local transit company, to say nothing of the National Whatever Manufacturing Company, where I am employed. They have stood in the way of my advancement because they know I am on to their little game. It's enough to make a man want to go out and boil a little blood or at least place a few anonymous telephone calls in certain quarters. But that is not how I got my black-and-blues."

"How then?"

"From listening to my well-connected, highly informed informants," he said. "The alert, thinking-type citizen these days gets a shattering amount of elbow nudges and thumb gouges. Like a man is sitting in the marketplace or saloon and a subject comes up—be it General Walker or Jack Paar—and the closest informant fills you in. He tells you that it is all an international plot and then he says, 'You know who's behind it, don't you? I don't have to tell a hip citizen like you that *they* are in control.' And the guy hauls off and sinks his elbow in your ribs up to the wrist. Or he says, 'It's all a plot between the National Association of Manufacturers and Walter Reuther, Madison Avenue and the Politburo.' With which information he delivers a fast thumb to your collarbone."

"I had no idea life was so difficult for you," she said. "You mean that everywhere you go people are telling you about mysterious international plots?"

"Not only that," he said, "but you can read about them every day and hear about them on the teevy. It's the newest craze, bigger than the bossa nova."

"What," she said, "do you suppose lies behind this sudden rash of international plots?"

"The only thing I can think of," he said, "is that it's some kind of an international plot. Why don't you just fold that statement and stick it in the envelope?"

Which she did.

"I don't know if this will help, officer, but he looked like a whole man to me"

I'll tell you, boys, this is a tough time to be alive on account of all the emphasis on the whole man. This is a movement that has been growing for some years now, and people who laughed it off and said, "Well, let George be a whole man," are now going to have to face up to it.

As is widely predicted, my expectation is that the ants—or some kind of insect—will take over the world. The reason is that insects are not always being bugged (come on, now) with injunctions to be a whole beetle or well-rounded termite or whatever their species.

It's the same with animals. If you're born a tiger the thing is all laid out for you. It's the same with a hippopotamus. Nobody expects the tiger to soak in the mud of the riverbank. The hippopotamus, similarly, is not called upon to pounce upon and raven small game.

Man is not so fortunate. Or not any more. A boy starts out and he is going to be a chemist, so he learns that trade and gets to be very good at it and invents some miracle ingredients and is happily married with children and a nice house and beer in the icebox and the week's teevy programs sitting on top of the set for ready reference.

Then he goes to a party and somebody asks, "How about Picasso?"

"Forget him," he says. "I am a happily married, beer-in-the-icebox chemist. Picasso is extraneous to my discipline."

"Ah-ha," he is told. "You are not a whole man. Ill fares the land where the inventor of miracle ingredients does not know from Picasso."

The same thing applies to the artist. From early childhood, he has been sketching, painting. He achieves success—a happy home, beer in the icebox, the teevy going day and night, his works being ridiculed in the best galleries.

At a party he is asked, "How about the neutron?"

If all he can come up with is "How about it indeed?" he has flunked the whole-man test.

Nobody wants to look at a painting which has been done by a man who doesn't know the difference between a Bunsen burner and the third law of motion.

Many of us are neither scientists nor artists, but this does not relieve us of our responsibilities.

This country was built by men who worked in the lumber-yard and read the sports pages and voted the way the precinct captain said. If maybe they had a few other interests, such as growing tomatoes or playing pinochle, they were considered to have been extremely many-sided.

Those days are going, if not gone. The call has gone out for the whole man—or none.

If you are not familiar with the latest in music, nuclear physics, pocket billiards, poetry, city planning, brain surgery, sociology, sculpture, spectrum analysis, comparative anatomy and psychiatry, then you are what is wrong with the country.

It would be a recalcitrant citizen who objected to this state of affairs. Nothing is clearer than that we must, as individuals, move forward in every direction at once.

But once in a while, as he turns from the loom on which he is handcrafting a rug to resume his studies of what's new in biology, preparatory to practicing Bach fugues on the re-corder, before leaving for his discussion group on "Whither Africa?" modern man may be excused a brief moment of rebellion during which he wishes the Cult of the Whole Man could have been put off for just one more generation.

I would purge from every published book every word that would give offense to the most high-minded (or evil-minded, if that's the way you feel about it) element of the community. No word that would shock or titillate the innocent, or send them running to the unabridged.

But, just a minute.

In the back of the book would be a glossary of all the words that had been removed, plus a generous helping of some other rousers that had never been there in the first place. They would be printed on gummed, perforated paper.

The reader who is content with the decontaminated text could tear out these sheets and throw them away. Others who would rather savor the rich vocabulary of the original—and even improve upon its lustiness—could separate each little adjective, verb or noun and stick it in a suitable place in the body of the book.

This arrangement would take a great weight off the police, the courts, the libraries, educators, censorship societies and just about everybody. It checks the matter directly to the conscience and taste of the individual readers where, I guess, it belongs.

We never sang folk songs because my folks weren't folk

As one who has known folk singing since the days when it didn't consist of much except "Barbara Allen" and "Go Tell Aunt Rhody the Old Grey Goose Is Dead," I suppose I should be happy about how well it is doing.

Still, I am not sure but what this explosion of folk music is not fraught with some peril.

A man walks into the home, let us say, and asks what is for dinner and his wife brings out the seven-string dulcimer, gives it a preliminary whang and launches into:

> *Burned up the taters—*
> *Don't cry, child.*
> *Burned up the pork chops—*
> *Chillun drive me wild.*
> *Eatin' out tonight.*
> *Yes, Lord.*
> *Eatin' out tonight.*
> *Don't take off your coat, Sam.*
> *We're eatin' out tonight.*

This can be a rather shaking experience for a man, so he suggests that maybe a quick martini might help him to unwind from the day's crises. Whereupon his mother-in-law leaps from her seat in front of the air conditioner, plugs in her electric guitar and sings:

"Martini to make me unwind,"
Last words he did say,
Poor boy,
Last words he did say.
Martini treat him most unkind,
Martini make him pay,
Poor boy,
Martini make him pay.
Martini make him unwound and then
Take the A.A. to wind him up again,
With a rum dum diddle-aye-ay—
Poor boy.

If the wife and mother-in-law have also taken to affecting black leotards and stringy hair, the whole effect is more wearing. A man could almost understandably prefer not to go home, except that if he is driven to hanging around saloons there are folk singers there that he isn't even related to.

Things aren't much better at the office. A man even looks like he is going to ask for a raise and the boss yells into the intercom, "Miss Duplicate, bring me my zither."

When it arrives he puts it on the gleaming mahogany expanse of his desk and renders:

Fat back sizzlin' in the fryin' pan,
Coffee cookin' in an old tin can,
That's all it takes for a happy man.
Look at that profit and look at the loss,
Shed a tear for yore pore ol' boss.
Boss got worries make his pore head throb,
Hear me talkin' to you,
Boss got a nephew want your job.
You get the message?
Boss's sister's boy, he want your job.
So get back to work, make them papers fly.
Look like a snowstorm by-and-by.
When we get a snowstorm in July
You may get a raise, now don't you cry.

The thing that causes the most apprehension, of course, is that the 1964 elections will go twanging down into history as the Folk Song Campaign. Already the civil rights issue is being immortalized in this medium, and we can scarcely hope that other matters will remain untouched, with titles such as "Bring Those Interest Rates Down, Boy," "Ol' Romney Was a Ramblin' Man," "The Sad Ballad of Rocky and Barry," or "The Higher the Court the Sweeter the Impeach."

An interesting and stimulating art form, as I say, but it makes an awfully long summer and fall in an election year.

Reverse English on the beer can

The editorial page of *The New York Times,* which always seems to lag behind me, has taken belated notice of my suggestion that the problem of roadside litter might be ameliorated by the introduction of the edible beer can.

It also goes on to repeat, as if it were its own, my proposal of some years back that beer cans be produced in colors and designs vernal, autumnal or brumal, so as to melt imperceptibly into the seasonal vegetation. (I don't know the corresponding word for summer, but it doesn't make any difference. In summer I think it is best for beer cans to look frankly like beer cans. This is the time of year when people are accustomed to seeing beer cans, and to camouflage them might be a blow to traffic safety, with drivers darting their eyes hither and yon trying to locate the beer cans that they know must be out there somewhere, instead of keeping them fixed upon the road.)

The *Times* does not touch upon my plan to magnetize beer cans so that they would cling to the surface of the car from which they were flung. Come to develop the idea a little bit further, how about a beer can in the shape of a boomerang, which would wing its way home to the litter chap who had thrown it?

(I do not like the word "litterbug." Why should the sloppines of Man be unloaded on insects, whom I have always found, disregarding the few mavericks in any group, to be a very neat type of people?)

I have even toyed with the idea of having motorized trash receptacles whizzing about the highways. There are those who feel that the neatest bit of courtesy of all is to drop the beer can into any passing convertible or sports car, leaving it to be whisked to wherever people in convertibles and sports cars go.

The trouble is that there is some thinking that drivers of convertibles and sports cars have their rights like anybody else. Be that as it may, the rag tops button up in winter and are not available as trash receptacles.

What I have in mind is a fleet of motorcycles or little Post Office Department kind of trucks with open side cars. They would come alongside and solicit your debris. On Christmas you might stick a dollar bill or at least a greeting card in the beer can in appreciation for the service.

But it occurs to me that the entire approach may be wrong. There is something about being preached at that goes against the American grain. Particularly on the subject of littering. After all, when our forefathers made their way across the land in their covered wagons they tossed out ladder-back chairs and iron soap kettles at every opportunity, as is attested by the prevalence of antique stores along their route.

A sign that says NO LITTERING merely offends something deep within us.

If we want to get rid of the beer cans, what we need is a Presidential Advisory Commission to Encourage Littering.

Secretary Udall and Secretary Freeman and perhaps the Ford Foundation and, if possible, *The New York Times,* should announce that the beer cans by the roadside are part of our national heritage and must be preserved.

"No pack of so-called alleged Harvard pinks who never met a payroll is going to tell me what to do with my beer cans," your Uncle Ed will shout, and he will put his beer cans in the pockets of his coat just to keep them from being federalized.

Signs along the roadside will say, the way the wildflower

placards do now: THESE BEER CANS BELONG TO YOU. DO NOT
PICK THEM. Whole carloads of tourists with fat ladies in torea-
dor pants and children of varying sizes will descend upon the
beer cans and fill up the trunk with them and drive off with
wild chortles and triumphant glee.

Whoever is in charge of the program to bring foreign visitors to our shores should point out that these folks will expect
to see beer cans by the roadside. They have read about them.
Beer cans will be as important to them as the Grand Canyon or
Disneyland.

The well-conditioned citizen will say to himself that no bu-
reaucrat is going to make him throw beer cans around just for
the sake of some foreigner who is probably from some country
nobody ever heard of but is getting his hard-earned tax dollars. And he will toss the beer can into his wife's purse before
he will contribute it to the scenery.

Conversation gets itself knocked cold

If people are really as concerned about the decline of conversation as they keep saying they are, then what they should
do is abolish air conditioning. In the Middle West we used to
have grand conversations from Memorial Day until the first
frost about how we were managing to bear up under the heat.

"Well," a fellow would say, "I drug the mattress around the
house until along about 3 A.M. I put it in a corner of the kids'
room and this little bit of air come trickling in over the windowsill and I got some sleep."

There was always one conversationalist who would say that
at his house there was always a breeze.

"Always a breeze," he would say. "Why, lots of nights when
people have said it was stifling I have had to pull up the top
sheet before midnight."

People would admire him and ask what part of town he lived
in, and when he told them they would say that, yes, they had

heard there was always a nice breeze around there, probably because it was situated so high.

The conversationalist would say that was very true. It was because his house was on a sort of hill so that the breeze—if there was one, and there generally was—could sweep right in his window unimpeded.

It all made for good, lively talk when one man could tell that he always took the hose and sprinkled the house every evening. This would turn out to be controversial, and somebody else would say sprinkling the house did no good.

But everybody would listen to everybody else's ideas, no matter how nutty they might be. Feelings would run a little high, but there was always a little central area of agreement. People would chime in with "That's right" and "Very true" when someone, a sort of peacemaker in the group, would say, "I don't mind how hot it gets as long as I can get my sleep."

Keeping the sheets in the icebox right up until bedtime was a theory with many adherents.

Occasionally the conversation would become especially piquant when a lady would admit that she kept her girdle in the icebox overnight so as to be able to make a cool start in the morning. Often there would be interesting discussions as to whether it was better to keep the place shut up all day long, with the shades down, or to open everything up. Families were riven down the middle on this matter.

There were those who would argue that a southeast exposure was the only bearable one, and others would take a diametrically opposite view.

I'll tell you, those were the lively days. Nobody talks about the weather any more because so many have done something about it. If you don't have at least a little, old wheezy box in the window, why, you keep quiet about it because everybody else has been refrigerated all night long and wouldn't know what you were talking about.

Even in the automobiles now there is likely to be an arctic blast from the dashboard and nobody wants to hear about how you drove across Kansas with a wet towel around your neck and one foot in a bucket of ice water.

It's nice, of course, to think about coolness becoming more and more widespread among our people, but it has sure ruined small talk.

¶ The air conditioner did more to civilize the Middle West than the steamboat.

"My boy's best subjects are lunch and career guidance"

Something comparatively new in the educational system is this business of having the bright-eyed young select a career and then go out to interview somebody in that field. I'm not sure exactly what the effect of this is on the student, but it can be rather shaking to the man being interviewed.

The trouble is that boys and girls today seem to be so much more articulate than the grownups—or this grownup, at any rate.

"What," the youngster asks, "do you consider the essential requirements for success in this field?"

The word "success" falls rather awkwardly on the ear if you have just finished lunching on a peanut butter sandwich from a paper bag. But it is complimentary and, after all, if you can't impress a ninth-grader, you figure, you are in pretty sad shape indeed.

"Well," you start out, "well, that's a very well-thought-out question, and I think that, well, you have to be, first of all, interested in this sort of stuff. You know what I mean? And then, well, being interested in the job is important and being friendly to one and all of your co-workers. And, well, that's what I guess would be like maybe the most all-important essential thing, and, uh . . ."

You trail off and look hopefully at your young inquisitor. His ballpoint pen is poised over his notebook. So far, you realize, you haven't said anything worth writing down.

"Well, now," you resume briskly, "perhaps it would be clearer if I put it to you this way. There are a number of what you might say are qualities that are essential and then there are some that, well, aren't so important as being interested in this line of work. From day to day. I think that just about covers it."

"Yes," the lad says, still not having written anything. "The next question is what sort of educational background does this career require and, specifically, what subjects should a person who wishes to make this career his lifework study in high school or college?"

This is a good time to take off your glasses and fiddle with them, while you gaze at the ceiling.

"Education," you say, "is, well, let's say that education is one of the things that are important in today's modern world. Very much so. The lessons you get in the classroom will, well, they will, uh, stand you in good stead. Of course, there was Abraham Lincoln—"

"What subjects—" he begins.

"Yes—I was coming to that—well, I think nobody can have too much reading and spelling and, uh, grammar and civics and, uh, that stuff about rocks."

"Geology?" he asks.

"That's it," you say. "Very important, geology. And the thing with the Bunsen burner—chemistry. And spelling, did I mention that? Also history and commercial law."

By this time you have the definite feeling you aren't being helpful, but you have mentioned all the subjects you can think of.

"The next question," the guidance seeker goes on, "is how do you organize your day?"

You realize that this inquiry has aroused the interest of the man at the next desk who is waiting in some amusement for your answer. You turn your back to him and speak in a rapid mumble.

"Organizing," you say, "is one of the best things to do to a day. I always, uh, every night I write down everything I have to do the next day. The appointments and the people to call and like that, and then when I come in in the morning, why, there written down are all the things I have to do and I, well, I do them."

Halfway through this burst of nonsense you see that the student is gazing at your desk pad where, under Things to Do Today there is only a solitary notation, "Lunch."

Often, after the interview is over, you are asked to fill in a questionnaire in which you rank the student as to neatness, courtesy, intelligence, familiarity with the field and general savvy. Almost invariably it is a pleasure to give him perfect marks under all these headings.

And how lucky you are that the judging isn't being done the other way around.

I'm in love with a two-job girl; moonlight becomes her

¶ An economic survey reports that most men who hold down two jobs do it for the money. I had thought they did it so they could retire with two gold watches.

¶ Stories of the versatility of a man like Leonardo da Vinci impress today's youngsters, who think of him as the moonlighter's moonlighter.

The administration has a rule that no appointee of the executive department can hold down another job for profit. It is generally hailed as a good idea, although some captious people are complaining that it is being violated by White House folk who write for the slick magazines.

What I wonder is whether it really is a good idea. If none of the movers and shakers of Washington are going to moonlight, how are they going to understand the average citizen to whom moonlighting is a way of life?

The man with only one job is presumed to have a rich wife. Lawyers drive taxicabs, actuaries sell air conditioners, and men schoolteachers stand behind the bar and mix the moonlight cocktail.

Wouldn't it be a good idea if the executive order were not only repealed, but reversed? Every member of the Cabinet ought to be not only allowed, but required, to have additional and useful employment. It scarcely makes sense for one-job men in Washington to administer the laws of a nation of two-job men.

There are observers of our economic system who are not enthusiastic about moonlighting. They feel that the man who has two jobs, or three, should cut himself back to one and let someone else have the others. But these critics might as well face the fact that we are a moonlighting nation, and it behooves our leaders to get with it if they are going to understand our hopes, needs and aspirations.

The man who sells you a necktie is a practicing engineer; the pilot who flies your jet airliner is, in the other half of his life, a coin laundry operator; when not ministering to his flock, the ordained preacher is a paint warehouseman; the nightclub piano player installs storm windows by day; the center-fielder is really a bowling alley proprietor; the advertising executive has a milk route.

We take all this as normal. Of almost everyone we meet, whether carpenter or professor of the classics, we automatically ask, "What else do you do?"

But no one asks that of Presidential advisers. It sets them apart from the mainstream of our society.

Wouldn't it make us feel closer to our leaders if, when a Cabinet meeting broke up, one Secretary went to shingle a roof, another to sell insurance, and a third to cruise the residential areas ringing a little bell and vending ice cream?

What it may take is a Federal department with full Cabinet rank for the Secretary of Moonlighting.

Do you really want to live on a street called Tinker Bell Lane in a village named Sylvan Shades? If you don't, you had better act fast. Before the onward march of the subdivider, old place names are being eliminated. Schwartz Road becomes Pussycat Mews, and old Schwartz's heirs wake up too late to do anything about it.

Bearing on this problem is a letter written by Joseph G. Harrison, managing editor of the *Christian Science Monitor*, to Rand McNally & Co., the map people. Mr. Harrison is, on one side or the other, a Mudge, which explains the emotions with which he noticed the designation Silver Pond in the northwest corner of Connecticut.

"Silver Pond, indeed," he wrote. "In the year 1738 my great-great-great-great grandfather Ebenezer Mudge moved from Lebanon, Conn., into what was then largely wilderness and settled near Sharon. He built a mill (known, not surprisingly, as Mudge Mill) on a stream emptying from what immediately became known as Mudge's Pond. . . .

"A few years ago, I am told, land speculators began moving into the beautiful mountainous area of Northwestern Connecticut. They soon reached Mudge's Pond. Perhaps understandably, they did not consider the name quite elegant enough to be the basis for a real estate development. . . . Thus with the linguistic taste which characterizes such individuals and their efforts, they hit upon the unique name of Silver Pond, little realizing, I am sure, that there are 2,000 or more Silver Ponds and Lakes in the United States.

"So, for a name which is today as much of a cliché as is Dew Drop Inn, Bide-a-Wee, Bridal Veil Falls, Echo Point and Vista del Mar, they happily and greedily ploughed under a name which, while perhaps not the most euphonious in the English language, at least bespoke Sharon's early and honorable history, a name which had lasted for more than two centuries."

This is a sad example of galloping cutification. We had better hold on to the grand old names of America—plain, perhaps, on the surface, but beautiful through usage, before they are cutified out of existence.

What name could be homelier than Abraham Lincoln? It is probably sheer luck that the cutifiers have not improved it, retroactively, to J. Byron D'Orsay.

¶ The West begins somewhere in the middle of Ohio, where the tourist encounters the first motel called El Rancho.

How about this, sports fans?

¶ American soldiers have always fought for the God-given right to boo the umpire. But when an umpire is drafted, what does he fight for?

Saddening to our friends, encouraging to our enemies, puzzling to the uncommitted nations—that must be the sum of international reaction to the spectacle of the United States of America, seeking in one breath to lead the world, and in the next demonstrating that it doesn't even know what its own national sport is.

Has there ever before, in the long and sometimes sticky history of mankind, been a great power which showed such indecision? At this very moment, when we are being looked toward for guidance, we are exhibiting an indecisiveness which would be amusing if it were not frightening.

A poll of sportswriters shows them almost evenly divided as to whether football will not (if indeed it hasn't already) supplant baseball as our national sport.

This seems to me to add an almost intolerable weight to the burdens of our President. Other Chief Executives have only had to weather Kremlin laughter over the fact that we were unable to decide upon a national flower, national bug or Federal dog. They have always been able to attend summit conferences secure in the knowledge that the nation knew what its national sport was and was unified in this regard if no other.

What good is it going to do to say we will stand firm on Berlin when we are advertising to the world that we are wishy-washy in a matter so basic as our national game?

I could make out a good case for either game. It is all a matter of choosing a yardstick.

Let's say, for example, that we measure it by the fervency of the nuts who attend the contests. Here we can argue that the football nut who turns out in 8-degree weather, drives 300 miles and sits in a blizzard has it all over the baseball nut who is discouraged by the mere threat of a light and intermittent shower.

Compare, however, how many Americans participate in each sport, and we would have to give the edge to baseball. There is hardly an indigenous male who has not swung a bat or worn a glove. Football, on the other hand, tends to be the special province of only the huskier young citizens.

Tradition, too, is on the side of baseball. We fight our wars for the right to boo the umpire rather than for the right to tear down the goalpost.

But, historically, who knows which is the older? If the Pilgrims had had a ball, would they have kicked it or thrown it? We cannot say.

In many other ways the sports are a tossup. They are equally baffling and unamusing to foreigners. This is a basic requirement of any national sport. There is no point at all in having a national sport that other people can enjoy. Half the thrill of a national sport is in its esoteric lore, the feeling of belonging to an in group from which the uninitiated are barred.

The fact that very few Americans really understand the finer points of either game is aside from the issue. In fact, it's all to the good. Any game that is to occupy the status of a national pastime should be surrounded by a certain mysticism.

Frenchmen, I have heard, do not really understand women, and yet their national sport is well established.

The thing we have to fix with a cold, clear eye is that it

doesn't really matter whether football, baseball or three-card monte is our national sport. The great need is unity.

In our glorious past we have always known that every American would fight to his last drop of blood if an enemy took the name of Babe Ruth in vain.

It is perfectly all right with me if we are told that patriotism now calls for us to take similar umbrage at any disparaging mention of Y. A. Tittle.

But we must coordinate. We must decide which way we are going to go.

Rome, as Toynbee may well have said, declined and fell because it couldn't make up its mind whether its national sport was gladiator fighting or chariot racing. Can we afford to blow the game in the ninth inning (or the fourth quarter, depending on how this argument is settled) by letting the world know we are similarly divided?

By the ghosts of Abner Doubleday and/or Walter Camp, I should think not.

Learn spying by correspondence: steam open each lesson

¶ America hasn't had a really reliable intelligence agent since Duncan Hines.

¶ Government employees are required to travel economy class on the airlines. No wonder so few of our spies ever seem to meet anyone with any secrets worth knowing.

As the books about espionage roll off the presses, it becomes increasingly clear that Americans don't rank very high among the world's spies. Hardly an author fails to give us bad marks in undercover work, double-crossing and all-round peeping.

Patriots are responding strongly to this indictment, and suggestions have been made that we have an academy of spying to close the sneak gap.

I must admit that the idea has certain attractions—the examination papers written in disappearing ink; the tuition payments tossed over the cemetery wall at midnight in used, unmarked bills of small denomination; the alma mater anthem so highly classified that it can be sung only in code.

If the spy academy's football team loses a game, the entire student body flunks. Obviously, a group that can't steal anything so elementary as an opponent's signals is going to have rough going on such future assignments as finding out the locations of missile bases and what Khrushchev has for breakfast.

It would be an ideal place to go to school from the student's point of view. If a fellow is working toward his Bachelor of Sneaky degree and writes home for money, he can tell his parents that much as he would like to tell them what happened to the last $50, they don't have clearance high enough for the information.

But, looking at all the angles, I don't think an educational institution of this sort would work in our society. The first thing they would do, in the American tradition, would be to hire a public relations director.

Every small-town newspaper in America would get a story about the local boy or girl in the senior class, along with a picture: "Norbert Glotz, Jr., son of Mr. and Mrs. Norbert Glotz of 1228 Shady Lane, has been graduated from the National Spy Academy, summa cum shush. His first assignment will be in Saigon, and localites visiting that part of the world are invited to drop by and say hello to Norbert, who will be disguised as an itinerant trained-bird salesman outside the Russian Embassy."

Then there will have to be an alumni secretary, whose job will be to keep in touch with graduates all around the world and print little notes in the news bulletin, hoping that those who are mentioned will remember the old school in a financial way:

Sam Subterfuge, '65, writes chattily to advise us to disregard press reports that he has defected to the Reds. He is really still an agent of the good old U.S. and doing his customary bang-up job while posing as a doorman at the Kremlin. "And Khrushchev is even paying my salary. Ha! Ha!" he adds. Same old Sam.

Betty Lou Bizmuth, '63, is teaching piano in her home town of Ong's Hat, N. J. "I was doing well in the London operation," Betty Lou writes, "until my mother cabled me to come home at once." Betty Lou says she still does a little spying but "only as a hobby."

Trickwell Treat, '66, has been honored by his superiors for his research in developing a tastier type of edible paper for secret messages. It now comes in six delicious flavors. Those of us who suffered through Advanced Message, Note and Map Eating with Professor Borgia will echo the official "Well done" to Trickwell Treat.

I think we can agree that this sort of thing would create grave loopholes in our security.

Maybe what we are going to have to do is check this responsibility back to the homes, where so many important matters are best coped with.

The American child, I am convinced, starts out with a natural talent for spying—bringing home little morsels of information about the neighbors, the households of his or her little friends, possibly significant conversations overheard at school or play.

American parents have discouraged this sort of thing. They have frowned on the talebearer and stunted his talent. The ironical result is that now there has to be a call for the investment of Federal dollars to reinstill in the child this natural snoopiness.

No formal academy is required, or even desirable, as I think I have shown. All we need to do is reverse our traditional attitude and, when the child brings home a choice bit of contraband information, give him (or more likely her) an encouraging "Tell us more."

It will not only, in the long run, make our intelligence agencies much more effective but do wonders for dinner-table conversation.

Is overvisit better than overkill?

(In these days of the exchange of official visits between the world's most beloved figures, can't we help ourselves to an imaginary one?)

WASHINGTON—A weary but beaming Tarzan, together with his lovely wife Jane, concluded his official good-will visit to the United States and other suffering nations today. The national capital capitulated, as did other cities on their itinerary, to the charm of the youthful, 70-year-old King of the Apes and his smiling wife.

Spying Senator Margaret Chase Smith at the edge of the crowd, he said to her, "You Senator; me Tarzan" and took her in his arms for a thrilling swing around the treetops of the White House grounds and nearby Lafayette Park.

At the conclusion of the trip he invited her to come to his homeland to live and she said she would as soon as she settled a few matters at home. Tarzan gave her a ballpoint pen which had been presented to him by Lyndon Johnson.

The turnout along Pennsylvania Avenue was similar to that which has greeted the popular tree-climbing couple wherever they have gone.

His brief remarks were interrupted several times by cheers and prolonged applause. He drew laughter from the crowd by his opening sally (which, it might be noted, he has used no fewer than 57 times as he has toured America): "Tarzan no speak off cuff. Tarzan no got cuff." Jane's smile won her a special tribute for gameness.

In the crowd were Congressmen in their quaint native costumes, government clerks, peasants, members of the armed forces, workers and small businessmen. He spoke to them, movingly, of freedom from time clocks, television, collars, trousers, electric pencil sharpeners, cocktails, barbecue grills, setting-up exercises, press releases, tail fins, money, casserole dishes and a long list of other injustices.

"We," he said, "want help you. We want all people everywhere live in tree. Eat banana. Talk simple. No clothes, no installments, no commuting, no taxes."

There were cries of approbation.

Turning to Mrs. Earl Warren, Tarzan graciously handed her a recipe for pickled okra which had been given him by Mrs. Lyndon B. Johnson.

Pickets from the National Association of Manufacturers, the United States Chamber of Commerce, the United Auto Workers and the AFL-CIO were generally peaceful.

Police requested that they lower signs reading TARZAN GO HOME but permitted them to display placards pointing out that the economy of the country depended on the continuing heavy buying of consumer goods.

A representative of the National Real Estate Board distributed pamphlets pointing out that local governments would be in financial straits if citizens lived in trees. Speaking, he said, for the nation's lumber industry, a man who declined use of his name said it was bad for trees to have people living in them.

Smiling, and seemingly unperturbed by these ripples of animosity, Tarzan gave the pickets photographs of Sargent Shriver and Orville Freeman which had been given him by the United States Information Agency.

He reminded the crowd that he and Jane had always been friendly to the cause of freedom and urged them not to fall for Communist propaganda.

"Communists," he said, "give you more rockets, more missiles, more same old jazz."

He revealed that his son, Boy, would head a Peace Corps which would soon be sending task forces to important cities to teach tree-climbing, vine-swinging, chimp-talking and yelling of "Ooh-aa-ee-yo-wah."

As the throng dispersed, there were only a few disgruntled persons. One middle-aged man was heard to say, as he picked up his briefcase, "It's just one more promise of help. It sounds wonderful, but we've been disappointed before. It'll still be the same old necktie, mortgage and why-can't-we-join-the-country-club after he's gone."

¶ Leaders of great nations have many important duties, not the least of which is touring the capitals of the world, greeting old enemies and making new.

¶ Communist countries are probably just as enthusiastic as we are when it comes to welcoming visiting dignitaries. Any apparent difference is due to our having more ticker tape to dump on them.

I am often surprised and delighted by the loyalties that lie close to the heart of the reader. Some years ago I commented, in connection with a news item about the existence of a St. Louis Browns Booster Club, even though the team had moved to Baltimore, that it was like stumbling across a tyrannosaur or a chapter of the Rudy Vallee Fan Club. (This was before *How to Succeed in Business Without Really Trying.*) I received a sharp rebuke from the national president of the Rudy Vallee Fan Clubs, Inc., or at any rate from a 15-year-old girl who said that was what she was.

It warmed my heart to think that one might see a 15-year-old girl on the bus and think her merely an empty-headed miss, dreaming not beyond Fabian, when all the time she is dedicated, through some sort of hereditary priesstesshood, to Rudy Vallee.

Something of the same sort occurred in re Tarzan, about whom I had written out of boredom with the procession of meaningless state visits that afflict the world's newspaper readers and without any scholarly research into the idylls of the King of the Jungle.

Here is a letter which I sparked:

Dear Mr. Vaughan:

If you will recall, about one month ago I wrote you a letter about Tarzan of the Apes. In this letter I explained that Tarzan was a British Lord, not the ape pictures make him, (I have nothing against apes) also his son (named Jack not Boy) was his own child and not one he found in the jungle.

Some people judge Tarzan by the Motion Pictures, which is bad for Tarzan because the Tarzan of the Movies and the Tarzan of the books are two different people.

Since the time mentioned in the first paragraph I have been thinking. It would show people the real Tarzan if a writer like yourself would read at least two of the Tarzan books. (*The Return of Tarzan* and *Tarzan the Terrible* would be best for this purpose. Reprints of these may be purchased at Katz drugstore on Main for $1.50 each.) and write your opinion of them in the Kansas City Star. Also if you would tell people about the real Tarzan.

I think that if people would read the books (and give Tarzan a chance) they would understand the kind of person he was.

Thank you for your valuable time,

Yours very truly, [etc.]

P.S. I hope you will do this for the sake of a great person—Edgar Rice Burroughs.

This letter is one of my favorites, and I really shouldn't

say that I am sorry I stirred the deep wells of Tarzanophilia which produced it.

It came at a time when I was discouraged about the written word, the libraries seemed to be principally interested in audio-visual aids, and magazines were coming to regard words as merely convenient fillers to stick here and there on the page to suit the art director's whim.

So, although the reader thought that I had been unfair to Tarzan, I greeted her as a *reader* to whom the Word was more important than the Picture, even the Moving Picture.

Without consulting her I have enlisted her on my side against one of the asses of history, the Chinese dolt who said one picture was worth 10,000 words, in answer to whom I would like to say that Mr. Shakespeare, in one sonnet, can tell me more about women than a whole gallery of pictures of them lying on their left haunch in front of a mirror. And in only about 140 words.

¶ HOME

IS WHERE THE HEART BURNS

It was our turn last week to entertain Fuzad el Nkrmh, popular local exchange student, and the family briefing session was, if I modestly say so, a model of its kind.

"Mom," I said to my wife, "first of all you have to get used to being called Mom and don't tell me your name is whatever it may be. Foreign students know that the American wife of your age and weight is known as Mom, so remember to answer to it and not look like you never heard it before. Next, I want you to domineer."

"I beg your pardon?" Mom inquired.

"Domineer. You're an American wife, aren't you? Before the kid comes over I'll write down a list of opinions for you to contradict. Remember to interrupt whenever I start to say anything. Ask me what I spent on cigars last week and tell me it's too much."

"What did you spend on cigars last week?"

"Not now. Wait until the kid gets here," I said. "Or rather, wait until you get here from your bridge game."

"What bridge game?" asked my wife, a slow study.

"American Moms spend their afternoons playing bridge. You want Fuzad el Nkrmh to think we are impostors? He has been sent here at considerable expense to two governments and three private organizations to get under the hide of real American folks. It would ill behoove us to act like anything other than indigenous personnel. You'll be out playing bridge and come in late for dinner."

"Who am I going to play all this bridge with?" she inquired.

"How should I know?" I said, with a trace of impatience.

"Do something; hang around the coin laundry, look in shop-windows, go over and have your mother let down some hems. Just stay away from the house until it's too late to fix dinner."

"So who fixes dinner?"

"I do."

"You?"

"Naturally. It's a well-known cultural pattern that American husbands do all the housework. Get me an apron. Nothing too mannish; maybe a ruffle or two."

I turned to the children, who had been absorbed in their own interests—serious-faced, crew-cut Norbert translating Aeschylus from the original Greek for his high-school sophomore studies; blue-eyed, naturally curly Alicia working on her chart of hereditary characteristics of gastropods.

"Alicia," I said, "your assignment is a simple one. Just stay glued to the old teevy set and whenever anybody speaks to you say something impudent."

"But, Father," she said, dimpling, "I don't know anything impudent."

"Your mother will work with you on it," I said. "The big thing is to stay with the teevy. Oh, yes, and occasionally when our guest from overseas is looking, you might get down on the floor and fail to do a push-up."

"But my gastropods—" She puckered.

"Are not as important as people-versus-people understanding," I said, not unkindly.

"Norbert," I went on, "your assignment will be to get yourself a ducktail wig, a black leather jacket and a switchblade knife. I'll borrow a set of hubcaps from the neighbors and you can run through the house with them as though the police were on your trail. Right?"

And that was pretty much the way it went. For my own part I talked with our young friend about pursuing the Almighty Dollar and made several carefully prepared remarks designed to expose my stupid misconceptions about his corner of the world.

Fuzad el Nkrmh said he had never had a pleasanter eve-

ning or one that would be more helpful in writing his thesis.
The only problem is that my family doesn't seem to want to
get debriefed.

¶ If the Household Hints columnists have their way,
everything by the year 2000 will be either covered with mushroom soup or coated with clear nail polish.

A cold bottle and a warm babe revisited

All right, so they have done this research which indicates that
the average baby doesn't care whether the milk is warm or cold,
just so it's milk. The result has been a loud outcry from people,
and even fathers, who have been up in the late and early hours
heating the formula, and now they feel that science, which
thought up this bottle-warming business in the first place,
should reimburse them for the wasted time.

I would like to demur. I have served my stretch of fumbling
around in the lonely hours of the night and heating the bottle
in the pan of water (before the era of the individual electric
bottle warmer this was, young folks) and squirting it on the inside of the wrist.

It did me a world of good. An entire world.

I am a better man for it. This country was built by men (and
an occasional woman) who heated up the 2 A.M. bottle. The
mistake of the researchers at Bellevue Hospital, whence this
report emanates, is that they are thinking only of the baby.
They say the baby would as soon have the milk cold.

But we must all understand that the object of proper baby
care is not, ultimately, the welfare of the baby. Although it
should be taken into consideration. The idea is to break the
spirit of the father.

Surely I don't mean "break." Gentle is a better word, or
temper, or refine.

The men who today are making the decisions about Cuba,
about Vietnam, about space travel, learned more about patience,

about understanding, about tolerance, while getting the baby's bottle to the right temperature and into the baby, than they ever learned at Harvard or Southeast Oklahoma Teachers.

The main purpose of the baby is to educate the father. Pediatricians understand this. If the child is ill they give instructions that two of the green pills should be given every 37 minutes and one of the red pills every two hours. The regimen does not injure the baby and does wonders for the father.

It gives him a feeling of importance. It salves his ego. If he cannot go out and protect the baby from bands of hostiles and packs of wolves, he can at least remember which pills are which, and keep track of what time they are to be ingested.

I shudder to think what kind of world we are going to have if bottles are no longer heated. The babies may be O.K. But the fathers will not have had the enriching experience of padding around the kitchen and examining the bedrock questions of their lives, such as "How did I get into this mess?"

Fathers who have heated bottles have learned a lot. They have learned compassion. They have learned to lie a little, as when they say, "All right, Sam, it's warm enough now," when it isn't.

If a man does not come to grips with himself at the darkest hour of the morning, when life is at its lowest ebb, and he is standing with one bare foot on the cold linoleum and the other on the windowsill as he smokes a solitary cigarette and looks out at the stars while waiting for the milk to warm, then he will never come to grips with anything in this life.

Now, at this crucial moment in our history, we are told that the temperature of the milk doesn't matter. I doubt the wisdom of making this public. Suppose that it doesn't really affect the health of our infants, we are still paying a high price if we lose an entire generation of fathers.

Some of us leading authorities are in doubt as to whether or not the child should be reassured by being told that thunder is caused by two clouds bumping their heads together. It will, perhaps, quiet the sobs of the nursery-age tot, but the trouble is that most parents leave it at that.

It is important, Mom and Dad, to remember that sometime, preferably before the eighteenth birthday, the child should be told that thunder is not caused by two clouds bumping their heads together.

Otherwise, the child is going to be taking an examination for his Ph.D. at Princeton or get into the Peace Corps or West Point or something, and one question will be "What causes thunder?" and he is going to look pretty silly.

Put a little method in your marriage

I have an intense and successful friend who is worried because his daughter is majoring in speech and drama at college.

"What good is it going to do her?" he wanted to know. "She'll marry a medical student like everybody else's daughter and what good is Stanislavsky and the deep breathing and the pear-shaped tones and the 'How now, brown cow' going to do her then? As an actress, a Tuesday Weld she's not. So there's no money in that direction. What will happen is she'll be going the all-American-girl route with the babies and the P.T. and A. So why does she need all this education in how to imitate a bunch of grapes?"

I said something noncommittal, as is the safest thing to do in these cases. There really wasn't time to get in a discussion.

But it occurred to me that the ability to act may be the most important quality a wife can have.

Take the scene where you have the picnic basket and the jug all packed and the children are jumping up and down in anticipation. Your wife calls the boss and says, "Fred won't be in today, Mr. Forbush, on account of he has this feeling that his whole left side is numb and he can't keep a thing on his stummick."

Well, a lot of wives will give you a bad reading on that line.

They will recite it like "I see the cat," or they will overplay it and begin to sob, or they will say that you have bust your appendix when the boss remembers that you got a week off only last year for busting your appendix, and he will check the company doctor as to just how many appendices a man can bust.

You take a wife who interprets a simple line like "Fred is sick and won't be in today, Mr. Forbush" like she is playing the ingenue in a road company of *Blossom Time* and you realize you have made a bad investment wifewise.

On another hand, a wife who projects sincerity in creating a role can be a great deal more valuable than one who merely cooks, darns the socks and shovels the snow.

For example, you are cornered in the living room by a salesman who is pointing out that because you are an influential leader in the community he is prepared to make you a sensational offer on storm windows for your automobile. He is saying that you can save up to 40 per cent on gasoline because the heater will naturally be more efficient if you have storm windows, especially on the windshield. Since you are a leadership type he is going to give you the storm for the rear window free and the rest at laughable terms.

Here is where the wife with dramatic training proves herself a jewel. She dashes in with her coat on. She is carrying an overnight bag.

"They're coming every five minutes," she asserts. "Dr. Nipkin says he'll meet us at the hospital."

Unless you are a real dolt, you jump up and the two of you exeunt.

It does the salesman no good to call, "You aren't going to bring that baby home in a car without storm windows, are you?"

By that time your escape has been effected, thanks to the training which my friend says does a mere housewife no good.

Listen to this. You are in a restaurant trying to figure out whether you have enough money for dessert. Your wife sees someone approach and gives you a nod. You look and it is the gypsy violinists. Three of them. They are going to ask you for your favorite selection and play it in your ear. Afterward, the tip.

Here is where you can be glad you married a speech major.

As the first gypsy rounds the corner of the booth she begins, "And another thing, Kevin. It's not just last night and the whole miserable fiasco and the lipstick on your collar; it's the entire last six years of treating me like dirt. That's it: dirt, under your feet. Mother told me that I'd never be happy with a man who wore perforated shoes."

"Your mother—" you may say. Unless you are yourself a student of the drama, don't risk any padding of the part.

"That's right," your wife will snarl. "Pick on my mother! How about your mother and the way she left the silver teapot to Irma after she told me a thousand times it was supposed to be mine? If you'd ever draw a sober breath—"

It's a difficult role for your wife, normally warm and loving.

But she does it superbly, and the violinists, standing there with their bows poised to render "I Love You Truly" or "Softly, as in a Morning Sunrise," give each other the expressive eyebrow and the shoulder shrug and move on to the next booth.

There they trap some poor guy who married a girl because she could make a soufflé. She was such a great cook and still they're eating out and the smartest thing she can think of to say is she would adore to hear "When a Gypsy Makes His Violin Cry," and it's going to cost him three bucks.

You and your wife return to a normal tone of voice and have the dessert even if it's 30 cents extra.

So you're way ahead by having a wife who can act. Even if on the way home she breaks the silence to inquire icily, "Just what did you mean by that crack about my mother?"

¶ A marriage counselor says that every wife must play a make-believe role. But is this any reason for her to put a star on her bedroom door?

Anthropologists think it is a Bad Thing to teach cheerleading to our coeds instead of more cultural matters. There is something in what they say. Still, don't our burgeoning women need at least some training in the fundamentals of enthusiasm? They don't get much of it in the classical curriculum.

A young woman goes to college and she takes a course in Shakespeare. This teaches her to be critical. She looks through the works of the Bard and spots every little understandable mistake he makes, like having a clock chime in *Julius Caesar*. The examinations consist of the professor giving her a line or two of Shakespeare and asking, "Now, what does he mean by that?"

Criticism is an important part of the well-rounded girl, but I am not sure that it is the most essential quality she can bring to a marriage. The average husband does not need somebody to point out that it was a mistake for him to put the ladder through the window while removing the screens. Nor is it really necessary for him to have a wife who asks what he means by whatever it is he just said.

The cheerleader reacts to mistakes in a different way than does the Shakespearean scholar. When the quarterback passes the ball to the other team on his own five-yard line, she does not call for a chorus of boos and nit-picking. Instead she shrieks, "Hit 'em again harder" or "We want a touchdown" or something else which, even though inappropriate, is encouraging.

The advantage of a liberal education is that it imparts an objective attitude toward the vast issues which crash and thunder around the ears of the citizen. But the husband needs partisanship more than he does objectivity. He is out there every day struggling against an opposing team that has him outweighed, outthought and outnumbered.

When he gets home at night, he doesn't need a well-reasoned discussion of himself versus the establishment. He wants someone who will meet him at the door and cry to the kids:

"Let's hear it for Daddy. Two steamrollers and a tiger. D-A-D-D-Y." Yay, DADDY!"

When he leaves in the morning, full of self-doubts as to how the uneven contest will go, it would help if a "Fight! Fight! Fight!" were ringing in his ears.

It might be a good idea if the anthropologists would knock off their generalizations and get into some solid research comparing the cheerleader as against the non-cheerleader when it comes to meaningful contributions to modern society.

Let's hear it for the anthropologists!

And I'll send someone for my things; but who?

Mostly I understand what goes on in the movie and teevy drama because both are tailored for the nominal mind. But there are two scenes I have never figured out, or rather it's basically one scene, but it differs somewhat according to the particular role of the sexes.

It is the one where he leaves her or she leaves him. In the first case he says, "I am going to my club."

Many an impressionable husband has tried this, storming out the front door into the rain, only to remember, while he is waiting at the bus stop, that the only club he belongs to is the National Geographic Society, which is in far-off Washington and, as far as he knows, doesn't have a spare bed. Being a husband, he has a total of 53 cents in his pocket and he has to squiggle back into the house in a rather wet and chastened manner.

Also, in these romances, the husband may pack a bag. Where does he find the suitcase? We are never shown. We just cut to the scene where he has the suitcase on the bed and is filling it with socks and shirts out of a dresser drawer.

Come on, now. You know where the suitcases are in the average home? They are in the attic and if a husband wants to run away he has to go up there in the indescribable mess and crack his head on the rafters, which is why lots of marriages stay together. If he does find the suitcase, it is full of his children's old arithmetic papers.

And where is he getting all that stuff to pack? The socks, ordinarily, are hanging in the basement to dry and the shirts are at the laundry. If a man has the kind of home that he can get out of in five minutes, all neatly packed, and if he can afford a club to sleep in, he's got the kind of a setup he'd be a fool to leave in the first place.

Things are even more unreal when it's the wife who is skipping out on the husband.

The exit line is usually something like "Sorry, Cedric, but it just won't work. Heaven and Mother know I've tried. Sam is waiting for me in a taxicab."

She walks out. Do you catch the unreality of it? No instructions. No wife can go visit her sister in Des Moines for a weekend without leaving behind field orders more complete than those for the Normandy invasion. I can't think that this infatuation for a mere Sam is going to change feminine nature that much.

It would be more likely to go something like this:

"Sorry, Cedric. It won't work. Remember Mathilda's dancing lesson tomorrow, and she goes to the orthodontist's on Tuesday. I've tried, Cedric, but it's too much. That stuff in the plastic pan on the third shelf of the refrigerator is the dog's food. The leftover hash is wrapped in foil in the freezer. Remember if you don't put out a note for the milkman he'll leave two bottles of milk and you won't need that much now that I'll be with Sam.

"Oh, and if a Miss Flange from the upholsterer's calls, tell her to go ahead with the green slipcover. Hadn't you better write this down? Good-by, Cedric, we had our laughs but it wasn't enough. I think the mayonnaise is rancid, you'd better throw it out, and send your gray suit to the cleaners."

She leaves. The disconsolate husband looks out the window. She sticks her head out of the cab and yells, "Tell the Porters we can't make it next Friday night unless you want to go by yourself. Wear a red tie with your blue suit and get Mrs. Damply to sit with Mathilda."

Cedric slumps into a chair. Minutes pass. The telephone rings. It's his wife.

"Sam and I are at the airport," she says. "When you open the refrigerator door, a little light may come on; don't let it frighten you."

An hour later she's home. Taking off with Sam just doesn't seem to be worth all the advance planning.

That's the way things happen in real life up and down every block, but you'd never know it from the silver screen or the giant eye.

¶ The wonderfully warm and reassuring thing about marriage is that you know that no matter what comes along you'll always have somebody at your side to blame it on.

From time to time, it is suggested that our nation's capital be moved from Washington to some interior community, where it would presumably be safer from enemy attack. But I'm warning you, citizens of Sludgeville, I'd go slow on accepting the honor, if I were you.

There would be problems. Just going across the street to lunch won't be easy, because some visiting Prime Minister, King, Shah or Imam will be receiving the compulsory ride around the block with a band, eight limousines and a truckload of photographers.

There will be all these receptions that your wife would be unhappy over not being invited to. If you do go to a party you will have to worry about protocol, such as whether if a Supreme Court justice and an Ambassador both ask you to pass the ketchup at the same time, why, which one do you recognize?

But the big burden will be psychological. When you wake up and suddenly realize you are living right in the navel of the entire world's attention, it is going to make you jittery. There will be no more casual flirtation with the news of the world. You will have to steep yourself in Cuba and wheat quotas and the Ways and Means Committee and moon shots and all the other gripping issues which you can take or leave in Sludgeville the way it is now, but about which you will have to have opinions when it is the capital. Not only opinions, but inside information.

I'd think it over, residents of Sludgeville. Not that I really expect the capital to be moved. Not soon anyway. There is too much invested in miniature Washington Monument paperweights, coffee cups illustrated with views of the Capital Dome and pillowslips depicting the Lincoln Memorial. Even if no more are manufactured, it's going to take a century to use up the inventory.

¶ Let's remember this—if the nation's capital were anywhere but Washington, D. C., the American League standings wouldn't be half so amusing.

The girl it happened to

¶ Only yesterday the girl next door was a child in a dainty organdy dress; now she's a grown-up woman in blue jeans.

The jolts that come to a naturally shy and reticent man if he lets his attention wander from the changes that are going on in our language can be traumatic.

I speak from painful experience.

At a pleasant social gathering the other night a wholesome matron, seated next to me, remarked, "My daughter has been lavaliered."

Now, I have always detested that standard scene in the movies where a character receives some astounding news just as he is taking a drink of coffee. The reaction, dramatic though it may be, is messy. So, bravely, I got my coffee down without choking or spraying.

My wife was at the other end of the table. There was no help to be had. No chance to whisper to her for advice as to what to say to a woman whose daughter has been lavaliered.

The word "lavaliere" was, in my experience, a noun. It was a thing that women wore around their necks—old, rich women usually.

What had happened to change it into a verb? And, I must say, a verb which teemed with sinister overtones. I could envision a rich, old woman being lavaliered by a cat burglar, entering through the French doors of the Riviera villa, grasping the necklace in his hand and garroting the unfortunate (though wealthy) victim with her own brilliants.

If this was what the wholesome matron had in mind as having happened to her daughter, she struck me as extremely calm about it.

The matron continued to regard me, steadily, wholesomely, evidently expecting some sort of response. But what? Desperately buying time, I ate an olive.

Never had I eaten an olive so slowly and never had the eating of an olive seemed to go so quickly. I thought to turn the conversation to safer channels by saying, "Aren't the olives unusually small this year?"

But that would have been cowardly. Here was a woman, one whom I barely knew, who had singled me out to receive this terrible (if that was what it was) confidence. Come to think of it, she had whispered when she remarked, "My daughter has been lavaliered."

The words were meant for my ears alone. No one else had heard. The responsibility for assisting this distressed (though wholesome) matron was entirely mine.

I studied her as I bought more time by slowly buttering a radish. Was there something slightly Oriental about her features? Some Chinese ancestry, so that when she said, "My daughter has been lavaliered," what she really meant was "My daughter has been revolvered?" No, no, there was that calm tone (even though whispered) in which she had spoken. Hardly likely in a mother whose child had been gunned down.

I had bought all the time I could afford.

I took the plunge: "Uh. Well, there's a lot of it going around."

The wholesome face brightened.

"Isn't that the truth?" she asked. "Veronica Louise says there are five girls in her dorm who have been lavaliered so far this semester."

And, turning to the man on her right, she left me to reflect upon this news. Or I would have reflected upon it if I had known what I had to reflect about.

The rest of the evening I avoided the wholesome matron, but it was not until we were in our car on the way home that I had an opportunity to say to my wife, "That lady I was sitting next to's daughter has been lavaliered."

"I know," my wife breathed, "and they say he's a lovely boy."

"Who's a lovely boy?"

"The boy," my wife said with some exasperation, "who lavaliered the lady you were sitting next to's daughter."

I stopped the car.

"We go no farther," I said, "until I know what lavaliere means."

"It's a thing women wear around their necks."

"I know, I know," I Jack Bennied (anything or anybody is liable to turn into a verb these days), "but the usage—to lavaliere, or to be lavaliered. What does it mean?"

"Well, where have you been?" she asked. "It's like going steady, only more so, but not quite engaged, as I understand it. The girl wears the boy's ring or fraternity emblem or something like that on a chain around her neck."

"And that's all that happened to the lady I was sitting next to's daughter?"

"Yes."

I sighed with relief.

"It's sort of like being pinned," she said, "but not quite."

I started the car, and we drove home in silenc
thinking her own thoughts and I resolving not to as
ing pinned means; not even to think about it.

¶ Mathew Brady covered the entire Civil War with
fewer photographs than an ordinary wedding calls for today.

¶ Indiana specializes in producing basketball players
and humorists. The Hoosier mother can be reasonably sure
that her boy will grow up either tall or funny.

Untamed lust ahead: proceed with caution

Bernard Oldpeople, just returned from his annual summer
auto tour, says he has noticed that the biggest change, over the
years, has been occasioned by the literary preferences of the
family.

"When the children were young and feasted on comic books,"
he reports, "the greatest problem was in getting past the snake
farms, bandits' caves, two-headed calf exhibits and similar roadside delectations.

"Not unnaturally, they wanted to check these exhibits, with
their promises of thrills and grue, to see how they compared
with the Monsters and Things of their favorite literary form.

"Later, in a spasm of teen intellectualism, their interest
turned to history. No marker, whether it recounted an unre-
membered battle in a forgotten war or the first soybean refinery
west of St. Louis, could be passed up. Each one, usually spotted
with piercing, last-minute cries which brought the family sedan
to a skidding stop, neatly peeling off layers of tread on the
tires, had to be read and duly noted in the day-by-day book."

"But," I ask, "this stage has passed, has it not?"

"Indeed it has," he says. "The children themselves have
disappeared into marriages and colleges and armed forces and
other institutions. No one travels in the family group now ex-

cept the two old folks, and the sedan has shrunk to a two-seater sports car."

"No further problems with the reading tastes of the passengers, eh?" I inquire.

"Don't be silly," he replies. "With the children flown, my wife has devoted herself full time to the lending library. Her specialty is the novel which tears the false front off the morals of the typical American small town. Behind the respectable façade, she has been informed by the writers of lusty, taut, frank, compassionate accounts of life on Main Street, U.S.A., lie all sorts of stuff that would surprise you.

"We enter a pleasant village, past the frozen-custard stands, the outlying automobile junkyards, the motels and beer joints. On the right, perched on a lofty hill, is a beautiful home, riding stables out in back, maybe a swimming pool, big columns, you know the kind of thing. 'Nice place,' I say.

" 'That's where the banker lives,' she says. 'Third generation. Drinking himself to death. His wife is flirting with every man in town. Their daughter has run away with the chauffeur. Only Old Sam, the half-wit (or is he?), knows all the scorching secrets of the decadence which lies behind the respectable exterior of the Big House.'

" 'Yeah,' I say, and we zoom along a little farther and there are some streets of comfortable new homes, small, well tended; tricycles on the front walk, you know the kind of thing.

" 'Unmentionable passions,' she remarks.

" 'I beg your pardon?'

" 'Beneath the smug surface of Gingko Lane seethes a veritable witches' brew of unmentionable passions, awaiting only the spark which can be provided by a forbidden kiss, a whisper overheard.'

" 'Yeah,' I say, 'look at the high school. Nice high school. And the kids. Boy, it sort of restores your faith in—'

" 'Thrown too young into the seething caldron of adult emotions, today's young people, in a rage to live, taste forbidden fruit and, well, uh—'

" 'Unmentionable passions,' I supply.

" 'Right,' she says. 'Let's stop for lunch, I want to see the sultry-eyed temptress whose kisses set a town on fire.'

" 'Where does she work?'

" 'Oh, anyplace,' she says calmly. 'Every small town has lots of them.'

"Frankly," Bernard Oldpeople says, "this business of delving into the abnormal psychology of every town we go through is about to kill touring as far as I am concerned. I'll tell you, it makes me yearn for the good old days when all I had to contend with along the way were 40-foot pythons and plaques marking the first iron smelter south of Pittsburgh. Who knows, if this thing continues, we'll have a reconstruction of *Peyton Place,* half price to the kiddies."

¶ An exhibition of the latest in home decoration shows a black telephone and a white refrigerator. What next, green Christmas trees?

¶ Kissing becomes more widespread as a meaningless salutation. About the only form of greeting which tends to be confined to the immediate family is the baseball bat behind the ear or the shotgun shell between the eyes.

Let's keep the real-life situations out of real life

You will find people who will tell you that the children should not watch the Westerns and the Private Eyes and the Medicals on the teevy, because all the shooting and killing and patients getting uppity with the interns sets them a bad example.

Maybe so, but what I would shoo the kids away from is the family situation comedy.

They place too heavy a burden upon the fathers of America.

What I mean is this. In the days when the cowboys were the biggest on the giant eye, a daddy would come home and maybe the sprout would say, "Bang! You are dead!"

Which is good news for a daddy when he comes home. It entitles him to collapse on the sofa and read the paper.

Or if the child was a devotee of the detective shows, he would say, "So, you won't talk, eh?" And the daddy only had to say, "Nope," and that was that.

In the case of the medical shows, the word from the young enthusiast was "I don't care what Dr. Zorba says. You're my patient and I say you're to have complete rest." This suits the dad entirely and he flakes out in the easy chair.

But if the kids have been watching the family shows, they expect a little more paternal participation. The fathers in these entertainments are always on the move.

One week they are playing the old ukulele they found in the attic; the next the boss comes to dinner on the wrong night and the mailman has to pretend to be the butler; another time they are boasting about being great outdoorsmen and have to go on an overnight hike and fall in a creek.

Through it all, these fathers, although occasionally angry in a comical way, are generally witty, understanding and forgiving.

It is nothing, in a TV family show, for a daddy to be greeted at the door by his son, saying, "I have asked Monica, Deirdre, Nelly Lou and Cuddles from the malt shop all to the same dance and they have all accepted. What shall I do?"

The guy hasn't even had time to take off his coat before he has to light up his pipe and give the lad a warmly human, insightful, poignant lecture about this situation. And he doesn't get the lecture finished because his little girl comes running in with the ukulele she found in the attic, the mailman is complaining that the butler's suit doesn't fit him and the boss is ringing the doorbell, expecting dinner.

Our children naturally get the idea that this is the way family life is supposed to be. Can you blame a boy if he goes out and gets dates with four girls for the same dance?

He figures the purpose of a dad is to give him some warm, witty, human insights into the problem and it will all work out nicely after a hilarious half hour.

In real life, however, when the lad says that he has concurrent dates with Monica, Deirdre, Nelly Lou and Cuddles from the malt shop, Daddy is likely to reply, "Well, Sam, we all got our problems."

And when the little girl comes in with the ukulele she says she found in the attic, it's a drag because he knows he never had a ukulele, in or out of any attic. The business with the mailman and the butler suit just never happens and if the boss shows up on the wrong night that's his tough luck; he can go eat at the malt shop and tell his troubles to Cuddles.

This is bound to lead to unhappiness, with discords of all kinds. The kids naturally think they have a punk daddy if he isn't whimsical and always falling off a ladder and can't even afford for them to have any kind of maid, much less a funny one like on television.

The child who is always yelling, "Bang! Bang!" or talking like Frank Nitti may not be the ideal child, but he is pretty generally preferable to one who wants family life to be a continuous round of cuteness.

Realism is the new thing in toys. A model jet airplane automatically ejects the pilot and his parachute. Equally realistic would be a scale model of an Air Force Public Information Office—press a button and it ejects a photographer.

Another realistic toy would be appreciated by fathers who have spent hours putting toy missiles together on Christmas Eve. Think of the thrill a father of this kind would receive when, upon opening the box, he finds a slip of paper: "NOTICE: Do NOT Assemble the 'Wombat' Medium Range Intercontinental Missile. It Is Now Obsolete."

Ask not what kind of a fool you are; she'll tell you

I am not one of those who want to bust out and criticize the mass media for all our troubles, but it must be admitted that they cause an occasional unpleasantness.

Like one evening this week. A husband in a tasteful residence looked in the refrigerator and started clouting his wife with a frying pan.

When she was able to request an explanation, he responded, "I am a fine man and have given you, as they say in the lovelorn columns, a lovely home and lovely children. Now, after 19 years of marriage, what do I find but Harding Clupferman's lovely egg in my lovely icebox. How would you like another clout in the lovely eye?"

"What do you mean, Harding Clupferman?" his wife indignantly inquired while applying a cold compress. "I have not seen Harding Clupferman since the Junior Prom at the State U."

"A tissue of lies," he snarled. "Look at the damaging evidence, Desdemona."

"My name is Francine," she sniffed.

"You are a Desdemona type. Behold the incontrovertible evidence."

And he brandished in the air an egg, extracted from the refrigerator, on which were the initials HC.

"I can explain it," she sobbed.

"Nobody," he countered, "can explain an initialed egg, especially when the initials are Harding Clupferman's."

"Well, Othello, old buddy," she remarked, buffing her nails nonchalantly with a wad of steel wool, "it just happens that the particular egg you are waving around there is hard-boiled."

"Not even Harding Clupferman would write on a poached egg," her husband replied. "What do I care how it was cooked?"

"It is all the fault of the mass media," his wife answered. "Here, I'll show you."

And, as is the way of women, who can always produce clippings when they need them, she shoved a snippet of newsprint under his nose.

"Read it out loud," she commanded, having once more taken the bridge of the family ship.

" 'Mark the letters HC on hard-cooked eggs when you store them in the refrigerator,' " he read. " 'It helps identify them.' What a nutty idea!"

"What's nutty?" she inquired coolly.

"This HC is nutty, that's what's nutty," he replied. "Boy, if I ran the stockroom the way you run this house, I'd be fired in a minute. You got only two kinds eggs, right? Hard-boiled and un-hard-boiled, right? So all you got to do is put an X on one or the other, right?"

"Which one do I put the X on?"

"It doesn't make any difference, as long as you know."

"Yes," she said, "but suppose I forgot which ones have the X on them?"

"Suppose you forget what HC means?" he said. "It could mean Hardly Cooked or Haven't Cooked, or Harding Cupferman, which is more likely. Maybe there isn't any hanky-panky between you two but you obviously have a subconscious twinge about him."

"How do you figure that?"

"I told you—the way he keeps showing up on my eggs."

"I told you—HC means hard-boiled."

"Ah-ha! Why not HB?"

"Ah-ha, yourself," she riposted, "you just say that because of Hester Blob from the Junior Prom, your old, fat sweetie."

"Her name was Hester Blaht," he replied, "and I cannot help it if her initials also stand for hard-boiled. You must choose between me and Harding Cupferman."

"Sugar," said his wife, "I just remembered something."

"What?

"It wasn't Harding Cupferman at the Prom, it was his brother Irving, and it's Kupferman with a K. Return to my arms."

"O.K.," he said darkly, "but just watch it is all. If I ever come home and find an egg in the icebox with IK on it, you're in big trouble."

So things in that home are in a kind of precarious state. All, I regret to say, because of the mass media.

The list of Ten Best-Dressed Women usually is made up of the same bunch, which leaves out the ordinary girl who can't afford the clothes. But the nation's hairdressers are on the right track in picking the Ten Best Coiffures; almost any housewife can afford hair.

All we need to do now is to broaden the scope and have lists such as the Twenty Loveliest Elbows or the One Hundred Nicest Fingernails.

Suspense and excitement would be added to the annual announcements. The way it is now, women just don't look forward to these lists because down deep they have a feeling they're not going to be on them.

Think of the joy in the family when, at the breakfast table, Daddy can unfurl the newspaper and cry, "By George, kids, Mother has been named by a board of chiropodists as one of the Ten Most Interesting-Footed Women in America, and Princess Radziwill didn't even get an honorary corn pad."

Send your proxy to see prexy

Another million-dollar idea which has just flashed across my horizon is a sort of talent agency for men who are faced with the prospect of going back to the old school for a class reunion. The fact might as well be acknowledged that most of us haven't turned out exactly the way we dreamed of 25 or 30 years ago when we said good-by to the ivied walls.

Those near and dear may love us anyway, but we are likely to be a shock to people we haven't seen for all these years—a shock and a disappointment.

My plan is to have a sort of catalogue from which the Old Grad could select a model to represent him on the campus. There are plenty of actors out of work and why shouldn't they pick up some extra change by going to class reunions?

Picture this. A tall, slim, expensively dressed man, a touch of gray at the temples, sporting a tan that speaks of vacations spent on costly beaches, goes to your class reunion and introduces himself as you.

"I," he will say, "am Charlie Huckleberry from Terre Haute and credit managing is my game."

Your old classmates will be stunned.

"Charlie, we hardly knew you," one will gasp. "Didn't you use to be a kind of short, dumpy mess with a big nose on you?"

"Yes," your stand-in will reply, "the years do make some changes, don't they?"

And he will eye the old classmate's balding head and spreading waistline.

The fading beauty who wouldn't go with you to the Junior Prom will be in attendance with her dull husband. Just imagine her regrets when you are there with your V-shaped figure and trotting her through the paces of an expert bossa nova.

All the while, of course, you are quietly at home receiving the admiring glances of your own wife as you snooze in front of the television. Your only effort has been the slight one of making out a reasonable check for your proxy's professional services.

Obviously the plan would not work in every case: If you have been seeing your old school pals regularly, or if the reunion is in your home town. But if this is the case, why are you going to the reunion anyway?

The purpose of a reunion is to see people you haven't seen since dear old Dr. Dedicated welcomed you into the society of educated men and handed you the wrong diploma.

Even if these people remembered what you looked like, they would have to admit that the intervening time could alter your appearance considerably. Any doubts they might have would vanish in a moment's reflection, when they realize that nobody would be likely to say he was Charlie Huckleberry unless he really was.

The agency would have a variety of types available. Perhaps you might prefer to appear as a shaggy, pipe-smoking scholarly sort, if only to startle the professors who were so free with their opinions that you were an idiot.

Entire family groups could be rented, too. These would feature, for example, one beautiful wife and three handsome, bright, well-behaved children. Think of how impressive they would be when compared with the families which your class-mates bring along, consisting only of such wives and children as they were able to find around their homes.

Nor would there be anything unusually dishonest in this plan. After all, the caps and gowns are rented; why shouldn't you have a rented image, too? And the chances are 50-to-1 that the commencement address was ghostwritten.

The land Emily Post forgot

Searching through the five-foot shelf of etiquette books which govern my every waking moment, I am unable to get much help on the specific manners that govern gracious (i.e., back-yard) living.

For example, when the hostess says, "Pray have a chair," is it proper to take a rag from your hip pocket (and possibly a can of scouring powder) and give the furniture a thorough scrub-bing before you sit down?

Or would it be more in quiet good taste to murmur something gentle, such as "Not a chance, Artissima, I got my new pants on?"

Some acquaintances are so Old World gentlemanly that they will sit when the hostess says sit, and never mind the condition of the chair. This may, indeed, be the politest thing to do, but the rest of the evening you are pestered with other guests say-ing, "Hey, Sam, you got a bunch of dirt on the seat of your pants," to which about all you can reply is "Aah, your mother wears barbecue gloves" or something else equally discourteous.

So we see here that courtesy, far from being contagious, may, in fact, breed rudeness.

A lot of outdoor furniture these days is designed so that you can't be sure what is what. When the hostess invites you to have a chair, is it gauche or *de rigueur* (one of these means O.K. and the other not, but who can remember which?) to say, in cultured tones, "O.K., Elmira, if you'll point one out to me"?

I have not been in touch with Amy Vanderbilt on this, but I see nothing wrong with it. Surely the hostess, far from being offended, would be delighted to know that her furniture is so complicated in the fashion *moderne* that a chair is hard to identify with the unclad eyeball.

Furthermore, if you don't ask which are the chairs, you are likely to make the wrong guess, and Norman Skeam, who thinks he's such a big shot anyway, will say, "Well, well, Sam, what are you doing sitting in the magazine rack?"

And you will have to say, "I am sitting in the magazine rack just to see if you were hip enough to notice it, and besides it's more comfortable."

In point of fact the magazine rack is likely to be very uncomfortable, but you have committed yourself and will have to say, "No, thanks; I'm just dandy right here," every time your hostess suggests you get out of her magazine rack and up onto a chair like everybody else.

Is it, I wonder, good form to take along a flashlight for outdoor dining? Most wives say no, but I can't find any recognized authority who has made a ruling on the point. The thing is that all around the barbecue oven there are little dishes of gunk or plastic squeeze bottles full of condiments. The whole ambiance, of course, is dimly lit.

Without the aid of a flashlight you pick up a bottle of what you take to be ketchup and squirt it on the hamburger. Naturally, it is the stuff the host uses to start the fire. Just plain old indoor etiquette rules that you have to go ahead and eat the sandwich, lighter fluid and all, and pronounce it the best you ever tasted.

Hosting an occasion of this sort is similarly fraught with problems of etiquette. When, for example, you drop the steak on the ground, do you brush it off or leave it as it is?

Does it make it better or worse if you utter some Old World gallantry, such as "Well, we all got to eat a peck of dirt before we die"?

Would it put the guest more at ease if you said, "Brush the steak off yourself, wise guy; you're the one who stepped on it"?

What about the neighbor who yells over, at the height of the soiree, "Hey, potatohead, no trash burning after 6 P.M., City Ordinance 9857, Paragraph 3"?

Do you invite him over to share the cuisine or for a fat lip?

These are all problems that you just can't find in the standard books that concentrate on how to address a duke's butler or what kind of card to leave while calling on an admiral. Let's have one of those bright girls who are always telling us that green ink is in bad taste come up with some answers. Quick.

The man who looks, however cursorily, into a shoe store window notices that the shoelace is vanishing. Some will say, "Let it pass; the shoelace has had its day like the straight razor and the drop kick."

But great traditions are involved here. How can we inspire our youth with the thrilling story of how fortunes were built on a shoestring, when they ask, "What's a shoestring?"

Families will disintegrate. The passing down of skills from generation to generation is what keeps the tribe together. I taught my children how to tie their shoes. That's all I ever taught them.

What will be the role of the father in the challenging years ahead if his status slips during the years when, formerly, he would have been teaching his children to tie their shoelaces?

Can we imagine that any child of the future will say with pride, "My father taught me to slip into a pair of loafers"? No.

Washington is considerably two-faced about this. It says we need physical fitness, but sits idly by while we are rearing a generation that will not have to stoop over and tie its shoelaces, one of the finest exercises, open to one and all at little or no expense.

I may be a voice in the wilderness, but when the shoelace goes, a lot of America will go with it.

In the happy family everybody can be anybody

One place where fiction is false to real life is that everybody in novels, even very long novels, remembers everybody else's name.

The Russian novelists, of course, change the characters' names every time they are used, and Natasha Tiomski becomes Natashki Natactovich in the next paragraph, but that is because of the language or the climate or the politics or something. The characters know each other's names, even if the reader doesn't.

Now, we know that in the home nobody is anywhere near as meticulous about other people's names as they are in the imagination of the novelist.

I am aware of a little girl who often refers to her father as "Mother," and there is no need to get Freudian about it or carry on in regard to role-playing in our society. This little girl knows the difference between Mother and Dad, no matter which one is doing the dishes. She just forgets the names.

But it is seldom that you read in a book:

"Mother?" she importuned.
"Yes," he replied.

Every family has a basic stock of names—Sam, Charlie, Ella, Laverne, Wayne and Lou (or Lu).

I know how fiction writers work. They have a big chart giving the names of all the characters in their book and they have it tacked up on the wall, so that when they want to write some dialogue, such as between Wayne and Lu, they look at it and Wayne doesn't get called Charlie, nor Lu Laverne.

(Incidentally, I have often wondered about a first novel. Suppose you have never written a novel and your wife comes in and finds a big chart on the wall with names like Beauregard and Nettie Faye and Clyde and Fred on it. She is going to say, "Take that thing down off the wall. The What's-their-names are coming to dinner. They'll think you are a nut."

It will do you no good to explain you are writing a novel, because if you have never written one before, your wife, quite properly, will ask, "How do you know?"

And, of course, you don't know. After you have written a couple, why, then you are established and you can tack anything you want up on the wall as long as it is bringing in a few bucks to pay the groceries.)

Sit in on a family group, however, and it doesn't go according to any chart.

Edgar will say, "Shirley, would you like a slice cake?"

And Norma will reply, "Thanks, Dan."

I'll admit this would be confusing in a novel, but what we're after is a slice life, no?

In my experience it is a pretty good sign of a family's closeness when Frank is called Jim and Sally is called Esther Mae. And without explanations. Everybody just answers to whatever name seems to be directed at them.

Nothing ruins the intimacy of the relationship like "Gus-I-mean-Glen, will you see if Judy-I-mean-Joan is ready to come to dinner?"

That sort of thing just slows up the easy flow of conversation.

Our talented fiction writers will never come close to holding a mirror up to life unless they recognize this basic fact. True, it might perplex the reader, but some simple mechanical arrangement could be worked out—such as an asterisk after the name: "Cecil*," and a footnote at the bottom of the page: "*Francis."

¶ The ideal family is like a democracy—one of those Latin American democracies where the administration will do almost anything to avoid a popular vote.

She's got a shape like a cello and a mind like an oboe

This man walks into the house and he is still reverberating. He has felt like a drum all day. The customers have been beating on him with big, rhythmic booms. And when he wasn't a bass drum he was a snare drum, and the sales manager was pecking away at him with little raps and paradiddles, and once he was a cymbal and got a big clang from the boss himself.

So with all this on his mind he walks into the house, or really rolls in, which is not on account of having stopped for a drink or two on the way home, but because he is still thinking of himself as a drum. (And because of the drinks he is feeling like one of those drums they used to have in dance bands where there was a light inside that would shine through and illuminate a scene of pine trees and a big yellow moon shining on a waterfall.)

Naturally he expects a little domestic understanding, but what does he see but his lovely wife slumped in a strange and terrifying posture.

"What is this?" he cries.

"I am a concertina," she squeezes out.

"How so?"

"It's in this magazine," she replies, indicating a copy of *Vogue*. "It tells how to be a lovelier you in a few simple steps, the first of which is that you imagine the lower half of your torso is a concertina. You compress the concertina by pressing your abdomen and the small of your back together. Then it says, 'Drop your chest into the concertina.' "

"Wait a minute," says her husband. "If you are a concertina all squoze together, how are you going to drop anything in? It seems to me I would open up my concertina if I were going to drop my chest in."

"You couldn't be a concertina if you tried," she wheezes back. "What you look like is a great big—"

"Bass drum. I know. The beating I took at the office today you wouldn't believe."

"You poor dear," she says. "Go out on the porch and relax while I fix dinner."

So he does, and while sitting there he feels like an Aeolian harp through which the wind blows, stirring now this string, now that into harmonic twangs. And he thinks over this bit in the magazine about ladies imagining themselves to be concertinas. The coincidence of it all strikes him. He never thought of himself as a musical instrument before. But here he comes home feeling like a drum, an entire percussion section in fact, on the same day that his wife is a concertina.

Another reason, he reflects, why theirs has been a good marriage. There is this kind of mental telepathy between them. A lot of men, he supposes, would come home and announce that they were a violin or a B-flat saxophone and their wives would ring for the mental health department.

But when you can share it, when each of you is an instrument, then you have a mature relationship.

And so it goes along, and every day he comes home and tells what kind of instrument he has been that day. Once he is a trombone when he has been slipping in and out of a rather tricky business situation.

"You can't be a trombone," his wife says, "you're not wearing a derby."

They both have a laugh over that. It brings them closer together.

The trouble of course is that she eventually gets tired of the game, and particularly tired of being a concertina, with her chest down in her lower torso, and decides to give it up.

This happens to be the day when he comes home feeling like a member of the now obsolete family of keyed bugles.

"I am an ophicleide," he announces.

"You certainly are," she says, and that's the end of the matter and she doesn't even renew her subscription to *Vogue.*

Now a distinguished psychiatrist says that pets are, themselves, excellent mental therapists. Many patients, he reports, are tremendously helped just by having a dog around.

I think this explains a dog I know. There are very few dogs who really feel that they are dogs. Some think that they are J. Edgar Hoover or Rock Hudson or Jackie Gleason. Now I see that the dog to which I have reference thinks he is Sign Freud.

"There is something about that pooch," his owner told me the other day, "which makes me want to bare my innermost thoughts. I come home from a hard day's work and I say hello to the Mrs. and I pick up the evening paper and lie down on the couch and the first thing I know there's this dog with a paw on my shoulder looking at me with those big, understanding eyes.

"I try to read, but I can't focus. I start thinking about when I was a little boy and how my father gave my brother a bicycle and he didn't give me a bicycle and he said if I wanted a bicycle I should be a good boy like my brother and quit socking my little sister all the time and it was a blue bicycle.

" 'Doc,' I find myself saying to the dog, 'everybody is ganging up on me at the office and picking on me and the boss gave the Acme Products account to that no-good Perkins who looks like my brother and drives a big blue car that I wish was mine instead of his and if my little sister didn't live in Omaha I'd feel like socking her in the nose.' "

This man, a perfectly normal, solid citizen has been worried about the way he blabs everything to that dog of his.

You can imagine his relief, then, when I explained to him that dogs are excellent mental therapists and that what he obviously has is a dog who thinks he is Sigmund Freud.

"What luck," he said, "to have a psychiatrist right in my own home who'll work for table scraps and an occasional bone. When I get home tonight I think I'll tell him about this uncontrollable fear I have of the water cooler."

The next day I asked him how the session had gone.

"A failure," he reported. "You know that storm we had? My psychiatrist is afraid of thunder. He spent the whole evening under the couch."

The best friend a boy ever had, poor kid

¶ Don't send your son to your old alma mater. Some of the most absent-minded professors never forget certain names.

He has gone away to college and I never did get a chance to give him any advice. I always meant to. But 18 years ago is, after all, just last week and there hasn't been time.

I intended to give him a lot of good advice. I could have taught him how to tune a ukulele and dance the Indiana. But it's too late now. The Indiana has died out. I was the last person who danced it, I guess. At least, I could never find any girl or, later, woman who would admit that they ever heard of the Indiana. After looking at me. I've forgotten how to dance it myself.

I was going to tell him a college joke which goes like this:

Frosh: Is your girl a good dancer?
Soph: No. But, boy, can she intermission!

It would have done him a world of good, socially. That isn't important, of course.

The important thing is studying. I intended to mention that to him. I had envisioned the interview many times.

I would be sitting there in my book-lined study, surrounded by the many plaques, cups and other trophies earned during a lifetime of scholarship, toying with (not actually wearing, that would be extreme) the hood symbolic of my honorary degree from the University of Leipzig.

"Son," I would say, ramming home a load of shag in my battered brier, "remove that well-thumbed copy of Herodotus in the original whatever from that chair and sit down. I am about to reveal to you the reason for going to college, which is to unlock the vast storehouse of knowledge . . ."

And so on for about a half hour of pal-to-pal communication, nothing preachy or pedantic, but meaningful, insightful and motivationful.

I haven't done it for several reasons.

First, as I have said, there have only been 18 years in which to get around to it. Then, too, the book-lined study never got off the drawing board.

For some reason, also, the plaques, trophies and other marks of high esteem from the academic world have been a little slow in coming. The University of Leipzig doesn't even answer my letters. It may have moved.

Now that the opportunity has gone unseized, I suppose there is nothing to do but look around for rationalizations.

And one of the best is that advice from generation to generation isn't much help anyway. The experience of the race is hard to pass along.

One reason for this may be that the advice one generation tries to give the next tends to be self-serving. We want our children to behave so that they bring us the maximum of credit with the minimum of trouble.

So we tell them to remember that money doesn't grow on trees and that colleges are for study and to do what the professor says and to behave themselves. It might be that the student who didn't behave himself and asked foolish questions in class and spent too much money on books he didn't need might get a better education, but he would be an embarrassment to his loved ones.

The discussion is, however, pointless. He has gone off to college unadvised, and about all I can do is to wish him luck.

Oh, and also call his attention to that bit about money not growing on trees, not to subject him to any tiresome nagging in the matter, but because it's such a well-turned phrase that maybe he might work it into an English theme or something.

Just in case he might find some such use for it, I have pasted it in the lining of his hat which, I have only just now noticed, he went off without.

If you write something pleasant about home and family, you have uncomplimentary tags hung upon you, such as sentimentalist and sweet old thing. So columnists must continue to limn the traditional picture, in which husbands and wives are perpetually in a state of war, or poised on the verge of same, and the siblings are locked in deepest rivalry when not engaged in hatching a plot against their parents.

Considerable sympathy is expended on the novelist. He writes his first book, which, naturally, is about the home folks, the usual set—bigoted preacher, alcoholic judge, nymphomaniac teacher, pyromaniac doctor, Lesbian seamstress, sadistic editor and homosexual barber. He grew up in a nice part of town, you notice. Mainly professional people.

Anyway, he can't go home again. Everybody is sore at him and wondering why he couldn't say something constructive, such as pointing out that the county has more window air-conditioners per capita than any other county in the state. But this only happens once. Moreover, with the book selling big and the movie rights bringing in a bundle, why should he want to go home?

The daily writer who has been pecking away at items critical of the American home *has* to go home, and not once but every night, to an American home. Without that movie bundle, where else is he going to go?

If he has made mention of hippy matrons or snippy children,

he may expect to be greeted by cries of "Why you—" and loud boo-hoos of "Hippy, am I?" or "Snippy, am I?"

All of which is why I have had to go to considerable trouble over the years to maintain the fiction in my own home that, by an almost unbelievable coincidence, there is a man with the same name as mine who writes in the newspapers.

My wife occasionally reads one of his pieces and says, "Why, the poor lonely old fellow. Nobody but a bachelor would write like that."

¶ THE FUNNY (?!!??)
WORLD OF WORDS

I'm sorry as I can be about it, but I'm afraid what we are going to have to take a searching look at in the following pages is Culture. The reason for this is so that the dust jacket can say that this book takes a searching look at Culture.

One plus factor you have is that when I am talking about Culture I am principally interested in words, so there won't be any pictures, which are always annoying in a book. You know how it works: The text will have something perceptive such as that El Greco was very elongated in the style (See Fig. XII) and you have to find the Fig., which about half the time is put in the book sideways so you have to turn the whole thing 90 degrees— always a bore because picture-type Culture books are usually big ones, so as to make a nice *presence* on the coffee table.

These pages, though, are about words and people who use them and what happens to them, both the words and the people, and if what ends up being defined as Culture by me isn't what you understand by the word, I just want to remind you that you are living in a society where a painting of a can of tomato soup is Art so let's not get too excited about definitions.

To welcome you to Cultureland (Free Bumper Stickers) I would like to mention the most serious use to which words are put in our Society, and that is Humor.

If we take one thing with more gravity than another, it is humor. The angriest panel discussions and seminars concern not civil rights nor the agricultural dilemma nor how many little black boxes are required to block the Bomb, but What is Wrong with American Humor?

The comic strip is a subject for psychological and sociological research; every nightclub comedian has a foreign policy, and the funny people of television are always threatening to be really funny if the sponsor will strike off the shackles.

I realize that "American humor, What's wrong with" is no laughing matter and have even kept a properly straight face while discussing the subject under respectable educational auspices.

The one question that I am unable to give an acceptably glib answer to is really outside the area of what is wrong with American humor. It is: "Forget about what's wrong with humor. What's it for, anyway? What good is it?"

My only answer is that I haven't the slightest idea. If the atmosphere is sufficiently rarefied, I may paraphrase the poets and say that, like a poem, a joke does not mean; it is.

But I have friends in the funny-writing business who carry a wad of guilt in their wallets which they insist on taking out and showing around like it was snapshots of the grandkids. They tell people who haven't even asked that we must have humor for such socially useful purposes as destroying tyrants (a technique which worked imperceptibly in the case of Adolf Hitler) or that it has a real combination-of-ingredients, fast, fast therapeutic value.

One practitioner I know takes a particular pride in this alleged medicinal quality of humor. He cites the fact that the *Reader's Digest,* a recognized compendium of medical knowledge, has a department which refers to laughter as your best prescription.

I wish him well. If the illusion that he is making people healthier by making them laugh assuages his neurosis, whatever it may be, I am certainly not going to puncture the bubble.

"Why, of course, Jester," I told him last time he brought the matter up, "everybody knows that laughter is the sovereignest cure there be for anything that ails the human frame.

"But I think if you are going to equate the funny profession with the medical, you had better clarify a few matters."

"Such as what?" he asked.

"Just as a for-instance," I said, "do you make night calls? At

2 A.M., the snow falling outside, the wind howling and the mercury setting new records for low, the phone rings and it is a fellow human being in pain. What do you do?

"The doctor has the Oath of Hippocrates and he whips out from under the blankets, saddles up the Model T and plows through the blizzard to the patient's side.

"How about you? Do you just tell the victim to read a paragraph from the *Reader's Digest* every two hours and come to the office in the morning? How about the Oath of Aristophanes? It would seem to me that you are ethically obligated to get up, dress and go over and tell this sufferer a laughable anecdote. After all, it is your theory that laughter is the great healer."

"Well," he replied, "if I am going to make night calls, I will insist on certain perquisites."

"And so you should," I said. "Indeed you should. I have in mind a special license plate or sticker entitling you to double-park while on a mission of mercy. When the policeman says, 'What are you doing double-parked there, Mac? I ought to run yez in,' why, you would reply, 'Officer, I am a fully licensed funnyman making an emergency run. There is a poor devil in there with a number of complicated ailments. Had I not gotten there in time with a joke about this kangaroo who walks into this bar and orders this martini, he might well have expired.'

"The policeman will touch his cap and say, 'I am sorry, Your Worship, I didn't recognize you,' and then he will turn to the assembled crowd and yell, 'Disperse and go home; this ain't no free show.' It will be a moment of glory."

"Only part of the job," the funnyman replied modestly.

"Another thing," I said, "is that I think you should be entitled to tell everybody how long you spent learning your profession. The doctor stills all dissension by jumping up on the table and announcing that he went to college for eight years.

"The funny writer should do the same. Suppose he has written a two-line joke and the editor says, 'I will give you five bucks for it.' The funny writer should say, 'My fee is $500.'

"The editor (being a layman) will say, 'But the entire joke

is only 38 words long and couldn't have taken more than seven minutes to write, besides which I think I read it in last February's issue of the *Great Northern Goat*.'

"To which the funny writer should answer, 'Typical of the lay mind. It is not the time required, nor the length of the joke. It is the know-how, acquired over 20 years of attending vaudeville shows and pool halls, reading the literature, studying *1001 Gags for All Occasions*. That is what counts. As to whether or not it is original, does the doctor charge less for an operation just because it has been done before?' "

My friend who writes funny was enormously bucked up by my suggestions, and I just hope he doesn't get in trouble the first time he tries to bust through the fire lines at some disaster with the explanation that he intends to go in there and tell a few jokes.

A salute to the unstoppables

On a peak in the high Himalayas two weary mountain climbers approached the hut of a Sherpa tribesman. Night was coming, and the menacing clouds indicated that a storm was about to break.

In front of the hut sat an old man playing tribal melodies upon a nose flute. The mountain climbers asked if they might spend the night in his hut. He assented and offered to share his humble repast.

"My wife," he said, "will rustle up some grub."

After thanking him, the mountain climbers entered the hut. There they saw their host's wife being embraced by an Abominable Snowman.

One of the climbers rushed outside and cried to the old man, "Say, do you know there is an Abominable Snowman kissing your wife?"

"No," the tribesman replied, "but hum a few bars and I'll fake it."

This is a joke which, except for the last line, I have just

thought up. It is the all-purpose, unstoppable joke. The trouble with most of us (or me anyway) is that we never get a chance to tell our jokes.

We start out and say, "Stop me if you have heard this one," and somebody stops us. There is no joke that somebody in the crowd hasn't heard before—and most jokes give themselves away in the first few lines.

The man who is stopped in mid-joke is an unhappy man, and unhappiness leads to all sorts of marital discord and kitchen drinking.

Go back and reread this joke. You have, of course, heard it before. Everybody has heard it. You have heard the punch line, that is. You have not heard the part about the mountain climbers and the tribesman and the nose flute and the Abominable Snowman.

I heard it at least 20 years ago, and the way it was then was that a fellow came down from the apartment above to complain about a man playing the piano too loudly at 3 o'clock in the morning.

"Do you know there is a little old lady sick upstairs?" he demanded angrily.

"No," replied the piano player, "but hum a few bars and I'll fake it."

Since then I have heard at least five variations. Each time I have been completely suckered in, as was everyone else in the group. We went right along, letting the man tell his joke, not recognizing it until he came to the punch line, and by that time it wasn't worth stopping him.

With this one joke, I firmly believe, a man can build a reputation as a raconteur that will make him a legend in his own time.

Have you heard the one about the President of the United States going to Africa to ask Dr. Albert Schweitzer's advice on the Berlin crisis? Of course you haven't. It goes like this:

The President decided that he should seek the advice of the wisest men in the world about the Berlin crisis. In order not to alert the press he made secret pilgrimages to philosophers and scientists, theologians and military strategists in all parts of America and Europe. They were all helpful, but still the answer eluded him.

His course was clear. He must go to deepest Africa and get the thinking of the greatest brain of our age. It was not an easy trip. Parties of engineers had to be sent ahead (in secrecy) to hew from the brooding jungle a landing strip that could accommodate the Presidential jet.

Finally, the President arrived. By jeep he made the last few painful miles from the landing strip to the hospital where he found Albert Schweitzer playing Bach variations on a mighty organ.

"Dr. Schweitzer, sir," he said breathlessly, "I don't have much time. I have come many long, weary miles to talk with you. Do you know Berlin is about to fall into Russia's hands like a ripe apple?"

"No," said Dr. Schweitzer calmly, "but hum a few bars and I'll fake it."

Do you see how simple it is? With this joke I guarantee that no one will stop you until you have finished. After you've finished, of course, you're on your own.

¶ Uncontrollable hysteria is a symptom of the dread "laughing sickness" which, so far, has been confined to certain African tribes and American studio audiences.

The American way: facilities equal but confusing

¶ Today's motels offer all the amenities of the best hotels—swimming pools, Continental cuisine, ballrooms and, if they get any taller, mail chutes.

The décor was elegant, the carpet deep-piled; the voices of the staff were low. I was in the lobby of one of America's world-famous hotels. A business acquaintance, resident in the city of which I speak, had called for me. He, his wife and I were on our way to an appointment. Someone suggested that it was early and we had time for a talk and a drink.

"In every world-famous hotel," I said, "there is a place where you can talk and eat some popcorn, and it is so informal that you don't have to check your coat or listen to loud folk songs. Such a place is usually called something snug, like 'The Elbow Room' or 'Ye Fleabagge' or 'The Bug in the Rug.' "

My business acquaintance spotted a handsome door on which was the legend "Gossip Room."

"This must be it," I cried. "I can see it now—the waitresses in pinafores and mobcaps, chandeliers made out of wagon wheels, English hunting prints on the walls, an Aztec motif to the ashtrays, early-American menus with effs instead of esses."

We started to enter.

In a flash of agility and black stockings, the chatelaine of the checking concession had vaulted the mahogany partition of her cubicle and thrown herself upon us.

"*Mais non,* you potatohead," she cried, addressing her remarks, for some reason, to me. "That is the ladies' room."

"Then why does it say 'Gossip Room?' " I inquired.

"*Je ne sais* cotton-pickin' *pas,*" she replied in a surly tone, returning to her post among the porkpies and Alpine-climber hats.

Challenged by the opportunity for social research, I asked, "If the ladies' room is the 'Gossip Room,' what does it say on the other one?"

" 'Gentlemen,' " she snorted, "but don't let it worry you."

I cite this incident only because it illustrates how far creeping cuteness has gone in this country. One wonders how much real leadership the world can receive from a nation which does not even have the courage to label its doors properly.

And, you people there in Washington who are in charge of persuading foreign tourists to visit America, if we who understand English, or had assumed that we did, are confused by this sort of thing, imagine how difficult it would be for the visitor from abroad.

I have always wondered how the tourist who knows only the English he has learned from a phrase book gets along with doors marked "Squaws" and "Braves," a fairly simple example of this type of whimsicality.

I trust that no one will think this an indelicate topic. There is no time for namby-pambyism when international understanding is at stake. Plain, understandable words are available to the sign painters. Visitors would, I am sure, appreciate their use.

The tourist from overseas who blunders into a Gossip Room may well go home and embrace, if not Communism, at least neutralism at its most virulent.

To put a fine glow on the whole matter, this same hotel, which glories in deriving its nomenclature from the spas of Restoration England, has a facility known as the Bath Room.

It is a cocktail lounge.

A lot of the unfairness caused by names would be eliminated by numbers. Many and many of us are working our lives away in routine jobs because we are named Sam Succotash, while a guy with no more hop on his fast ball is sitting behind a vast expanse of mahogany, merely because he has a name like F. Montpelier Yaksaddle which looks good on the firm's letterhead. If we were numbered 86289 and he was 97204, it would be more equal. Right?

Here is another bad thing about names. You meet somebody and he says usen't you to live in Fargo, North Dakota, and have a redheaded sister that played the piano and whatever happened to her? If you say no, he says it was somebody with a name a whole lot like yours—Wambly or Norcross, something like that.

All numbers sound pretty much alike, so he isn't going to start up anything with you about having known somebody with a number similar to yours. If he wants to tell you about a redhead in Fargo, North Dakota, he can come right out about it without all that cover-up about it being your sister.

I think if people would consider it impartially, many of

them would just as soon be numbered as named, and if so, it's time for them to stand up and be counted.

A gentleman is always nicely dictionaried

A news source reports that an unnamed public utility in a large city refers, in its advertisements, to "the well-telephoned house." This means, I would judge, a house with enough telephones—somewhere in the vicinity of 85. The news source was citing this as an example of the debasement of the language. The telephoned home, this source feels, is an unfortunate expression.

Not at all.

It is merely an extension of a trend in our language which should be applauded as a time-saver, a boon to courtesy and an all-round contribution to the fogginess of expression which is so necessary today.

I got the word just in time, as a matter of fact, to save me from embarrassment. Friends were showing us through their new home. I thought the furnishings were abominable, the color scheme wretched, the titles on the bookshelves lamentable. More than that, I caught some dust under a window ledge and, when nobody was around, a grievously unpaid bill in the escritoire drawer.

Now when this friend said, "How do you like my costly home, Sam?" I might have been hard put to find something to say.

As it was, I soothed a cuticle and murmured, "It seems to be very thoroughly telephoned."

It went over very well. The friend felt complimented—as, indeed, he should have—and I was relieved of any obligation to say, "Well, the mauve of the fireside chair don't seem to pick up the taupe of the billiard table for you very much there, Norm," an observation which might have caused strain.

I rather look forward to the campaign biography of the future: "Although he grew up in a humble home, it was well-telephoned."

We might as well all start talking this way, since it obviously is the wave of the future.

Meet someone at a party, and you inquire, "Say, lady, are you well-childrened around your house?"

"Yes," she will reply, "we are babied, toddlered and teen-agered."

Fall heavily to the ground upon entering your own residence and you can say to the assembled family, "I wish this front hall weren't quite so well roller-skated."

Slam your fist upon the desk and yell to your wife, "The trouble with this family is, it is over-steaked, over-automobiled, over-minked, over-shod, over-schooled and under-financed."

A while back when the electricity in my own home used to stage ominous demonstrations, an electrician told me that we were under-watted and over-fused. It started me looking around the place and I noticed that we were over-booked, only adequately telephoned, over-magazined, well-basketballed and under-easy-chaired.

In the language of the day a man who turns down an invitation to play poker says, "Well, uh, the fact is that at the moment I am just a little bit over-wifed."

The little woman no longer asks if you are ready for more coffee. She says, "Are you well-coffeed?" Friends invite you, "Come spend a week; the house is well-bedroomed."

"What do you mean you didn't know what time it was?" a husband shouts. "The house is well-clocked."

It is all encouraging evidence that, as a people, we are well-languaged.

This has to be the twilight of rhetoric

You couldn't be wronger if you think that I am an expert on the grammatical intricacies of what has to be the most important current trend in the American language.

I am tempted to call it the Madison Avenue imperative, but why keep hitting poor old Madison Avenue over the head? It has been buffeted enough for messing us up languagewise, by introducing "wise" as a suffix and other crimes of which it is no more guilty than many another thoroughfare.

Whatever it is, I am beginning to rebel against it.

For example, someone will ask me to listen to an operatic recording.

"This," he says, "has to be the greatest soprano voice of the twentieth century."

Heretofore, I have been spineless and said, "Yeah. Nice little voice she's got going for her there," or something else which at least conforms to the rules of classical rhetoric.

But from now on, I'm going to say, "What do you mean it *has* to be? Are you implying that somebody is forcing this woman to have the greatest soprano voice of the twentieth century? If so, what's his name? Sam Svengali? Take him downtown and book him."

The sports announcers do it, and they go further. They intrude upon my own personal opinions and even want to rewrite my life for me.

"This has to be the greatest third quarter you have ever seen, sports fan," one told me the other Saturday. Why does it *have* to be? How does he know how many great third quarters I have seen? And even if he did, how does he know I have never seen a greater one? And isn't my opinion as good as his? Is this a free country or have we already knuckled under?

"Fred," one of the sportscasting team will say to the other, "don't you agree that Slashing Sam Sausage has to be one of the finest gentlemen in the game today?"

"Nat," says his partner, "he has to be."

So where's the credit for the gentleman? Anybody can be a gentleman if he has to be.

It's spreading, friends, it has to be spreading.

And what can ruin a day quicker?

The wife confronts you at the breakfast table.

"This must be the greatest November 9 in history," she says. "Look at that sunshine. It has to be the greatest."

"You better believe it," chips in a child.

"You couldn't be righter," adds a second.

Well, what is there left for you to do but pick at the grape-fruit and mutter? You want to ask why it "must" be the greatest. Who has given the orders?

But do you dare say anything about it? The child who said, "You better believe it," is heavily muscled and skilled in karate. Would he splinter his own father with the edge of a palm the way he does a plank? Would anyone say, "You better believe it," unless there was a threat behind it?

Probably, and prudently, you'd better believe it.

And that last one, about "You couldn't be righter." A 7-year-old girl. How does she know how right you could be, if only you had a chance?

Tough times lie ahead; they have to. Literature and elo-quence require rewriting:

"She's got to walk in beauty like the night . . ."

". . . a pause in the day's occupation that has to be known as the children's hour . . ."

"And now you better believe he belongs to the ages."

This fad, of course, has to pass, but meanwhile you better believe that these have got to be the times that must try men's souls.

My little boy is more primitive than your little boy

¶ An artist can get by with a primitive technique if he has a sophisticated agent.

The primitive is the big thing in art circles these days, but why should it be limited to cultural concerns?

"I would like for you to come out to the house for dinner," a friend well might say. "My wife is a primitive cook. Her work bears the same resemblance to ordinary, edible food as the sculptures of the Aucan Indians of Venezuela do to the works of Rodin.

"That is why I think you will find the meal fascinating. You will enjoy the superb, direct vigor with which she attacks a potato, for example. There are none of the sauces and seasonings of an effete civilization—just the basic, earthy potato, semicooked."

Or we might write a note to the teacher: "My son Newton complains that you have been speaking unkindly of his arithmetic. You must realize that Newton is a practitioner of primitive mathematics. He goes back to an early day before fractions and decimals and things like that spoiled the clear, unsullied vision of the dawn of civilization.

"Newton's mother and I are naturally worried that too much instruction will destroy the primitive purity of his addition and subtraction."

Much is made over the amateur Sunday painter because he is a primitive. If, that is, what he is painting is landscapes or portraits.

But let a man paint a wall or a bookcase or the living room ceiling in a messy manner and all he gets is hoots and derision from the assembled family and neighbors.

It is a strange flaw in the character of the modern businessman that he will hang on his wall a reproduction of a cave drawing from southern France, a ritual mask of the Trobriand Islanders and an Aztec painting, and yet will react strongly against other aspects of primitivism.

I would like to imagine P. J. Woolgather, collector of primitive artifacts and president of the Unendurable Steel Company, calling up a fellow art-lover and tycoon.

"Exciting news," he would say. "My secretary, Miss Slantbar, has been on vacation and they sent me a girl from the secretarial pool who is the most primitive typist I have come across in a half century.

"She is the Grandma Moses of the typewriter. Only 19 years old and yet she types as though she had been born centuries before the typewriter was invented—or the English language, for that matter.

"I'm sending her work to Hofstatter at the museum. I think it's strongly influenced by the work of the Peruvian primitives.

And get this—when I called her in, the poor girl was almost in tears. She promised to do better.

" 'Don't ever change, my child,' I said. 'I can get typists by the dozen who type in the modern manner. This office is full of typists who can operate the shift lever and put margins on letters and even spell. You, my child, have the fresh, pristine quality of an ancient and disappearing race.' "

But, of course, he won't do it. And if he did, the girl probably wouldn't appreciate the compliment.

It hardly seems fair that the artist is able to get away with imitating the primitives, while about all it would get people in other lines of work is fired.

¶ History shrouds the exact date when the wheel was invented, but it couldn't have come too soon for the man who had invented the axle but didn't know why.

Closing the gag gap

Research Review, a publication of the Office of Aerospace Research, discloses that the Air Force is underwriting research into the value of wit in situations of military stress. "It has . . . been noted," the report says, "that the wit or 'funny guy' can frequently relieve tension, raise morale and increase efficiency of group or unit . . . by his humorous or sarcastic remarks. . . . The deliberate wit is present in groups whose morale and efficiency are significantly higher."

(Let us, on the basis of this research, look ahead to a news item a few years hence.)

WASHINGTON, May 4—Lt. Gen. William J. (Sliding Billy) Flooglestreet, the Pentagon's Chief of Funny, today defended before a Senate investigating committee the policies of his department, which is charged with maintaining the nation's humor posture in a ready condition.

Senator Trauma (D., Mo.) said his private intelligence sources indicated that Russia had inaugurated a crash program for funny and now enjoyed a considerable lead.

"The wit lag," said the Senator, "must be closed, or our grandchildren will be telling jokes about samovars and 'a funny thing happened to me on the way to Minsk.' "

General Flooglestreet, who displayed four rows of ribbons earned in his years of leading the nation's armed services to what most citizens had thought were impregnably funny heights, protested that the Senator was confusing the statistics.

"We are concentrating," he said, "on the anti-joke joke. Any time an enemy launches a funny attack on us, we are prepared for massive retaliation within 15 minutes. We have enough ad libs for 20 years stockpiled in caves."

Senator Dilemma (R., Iowa) interrupted to pay a glowing tribute to the witness's accomplishments in wit, both offensive and defensive.

He reminded the crowded hearing room that it was Flooglestreet who had headed up the old supersecret Bureau of Funny in the darkest days of World War II.

"Many people fail to realize," the Senator said, "that it was Flooglestreet who designed the Pentagon. Plans for a four-sided building had been approved, when General Flooglestreet, although then only a major, pointed out how much funnier it would be if it had five sides.

"The rest, of course, is history. Wherever Americans have been under conditions of stress, the mere mention of the Pentagon has been good for a relaxing chuckle."

Under questioning, General Flooglestreet said that personnel was one of his division's recurring problems.

"It is very hard to get a skilled funny technician to remain in uniform," he said. "Every week we lose our funniest noncoms to civilian life, as television comedians, traffic engineers and candidates for the Senate. Selling a career in the funny corps is a difficult one when we cannot compete with civilian salaries."

Senator Anathema (D., Miss.) said that one of his constituents, although certified by his high school principal and Congressman as one of the funniest young men in Yazoo City, had been on kitchen police ever since his induction.

General Flooglestreet said he thought that all Americans would realize that it was a long-established tradition for our armed services to put its funniest soldiers on K.P.

"If," he said, "we ever get to the point where we cannot assign our finest, most deliberate wits, to kitchen police, then the army will not be the army that I have known and loved."

He said that the Defense Department's Funny Academy at Yucca Flats was being expanded.

"In the space age," he testified, "we cannot rely on random, ill-timed or merely tactical witticisms. We must know that our long-term, strategic plans are genuinely sidesplitting. In the funny race there is no runner-up."

As he left the stand, the general slipped on an M-1 banana peel and received a round of mild applause and a few giggles.

Creativity is the magic word in business these days. Top management had better think creatively or it will hear from dissatisfied stockholders. The sales manager seeks to imbue his staff with the spirit of creative salesmanship.

There are signs that Madison Avenue is becoming a bit disenchanted with the word "creative." The trouble, apparently, is that it has become associated, in the specialized world of the communicators, with advertisements that are terribly arty but don't necessarily move the goods.

Well, the advertising people can retreat from the creative frontier if they want to, but they are bucking a trend. The word is too useful to be abandoned. The plain lie in politics is gracefully explained away as merely an example of creative statistics. Any day now I expect a defaulting cashier to say that what he did was not embezzlement but creative bookkeeping.

¶ A matter of historical speculation: Could Michelangelo, lying there on his back, painting the ceiling, have imagined that someday a cook who put anchovies in an avocado dip would be called creative?

Is a fe.w more than a f.ew?

The inch and the pound and the mile and other comfy measurements are on their way out, or at least that is the way the engineers hope that things are trending. They are too inaccurate. As somebody pointed out the other afternoon when a bunch of us were sitting around, the inch, which used to be 25.4000508 millimeters, has been rounded off to 25.4 millimeters, which means the inch is two-millionths of an inch shorter and you can see what this would do to aircraft tolerances to say nothing of the measuring of basketball players.

Engineering friends want to put everything on the metrical system and I can grasp their point. It is undoubtedly galling for them when they are grinding a valve and they ask, "Hey, Mac, how big a hole you want ground in this valve?" and the guy answers, "Oh, you know, about so big."

Too much of this sort of thing and the balloon doesn't go up.

Still, once the metric system is established for all the really important things in life, such as the bomb and exploring outer space, the other, admittedly sloppy, measurements should be left for us to use around the house and in the rub of our day-to-day transactions.

Because the very charm of the units of measurement which most of us use lies in their inaccuracy. For example, if you stop and ask a fellow who is leaning against a gasoline pump at Nevermind Crossroads, Alabama, how far he reckons it is to East Wherever, he will say that he reckons it at two miles, give or take a few.

Now, he doesn't know that it's two miles, and you know he doesn't, and he knows that you know he doesn't. This is poetry. It is in the realm of fantasy, and whether or not it would be better if he said it was 2.6 kilometers depends on which you think is more important—poetry or knowing exactly how far it is where you are going.

Consider this:

You are carrying your mother-in-law's suitcase in from the car at the start of her two-week visit, and you say, "Boy, Mom, that must weigh about a ton."

It doesn't weigh anywhere near a ton. You are expressing an attitude, and she knows it. A suitcase weighing exactly the same, if it belongs to some little old, big-eyed young thing, why, you'll heft it onto the bus for her and say, "Shucks, ma'am, why, that bag of yours must be full of feathers, why, it couldn't weight no more than a couple a ounces." And you've slipped your disk but you keep quiet about it.

Millimeters and so on are all right, but there's no passion in them. Like when somebody says, "Hey, I remember when Babe Ruth pointed over the fence that time and hit that home run, why, it landed just an inch from where I was sitting."

No such thing happened, but inch is a word that we understand. If you translated it into millimeters you've taken the heart out of it.

And then we have all these adjectives we apply to units of measure. The sportscaster will say, "He missed it by a good foot, fans," or we'll say, "Man, this cottage we had was about a country mile from the swimming pool," or a manufacturer will say the screens on his TV sets are 21 generous inches. Tell me what engineer is going to reduce a good foot, a country mile or a generous inch into meters or decimals thereof?

What is several, a few, a lot, a dab, a dollop, a bunch? What is a second when a woman says that's what she'll be ready in? Or an hour when it lasts 30 minutes on TV?

We all learn from experience what these things are, and I have to agree they aren't much good for science (you couldn't build an atom bomb, I suppose, with a recipe calling for two pinches of uranium and a smidgeon of heavy water), but they are so thoroughly intertwined in our thinking that I doubt if they can ever be completely rooted out.

The moon is new and you're so executive

Does anybody remember the great words, the ones that thrilled and challenged, that rang with the sound of trumpets and the unbearable clash of cymbals? Words such as imperial, de luxe, royal, aristocrat, Fifth Avenue, you know the ones I mean, full of implications of being special, a cut above the ordinary run of things, custom- made, high-priced?

They are all gone now, replaced by a single adjective (also, on occasion, a noun or adverb).

I refer to "executive."

The other day, without looking at the menu, as is the way with us gourmets, I indicated that I would have the Cheeseburger Supreme. I know what a Cheeseburger Supreme is. It has a slice of tomato and a pickle and a fistful of potato chips and if it cost 10 cents more than the ordinary Cheeseburger, we gourmets count it a dime well spent.

"We do not have the Cheeseburger Supreme," said the waitress as if she had never heard the expression before.

"O.K.," I said. "Bring me the ordinary cheeseburger with a slice of tomato, pickle and fistful of potato chips."

"Ah-hah," she cried, "you mean the Executive Cheeseburger."

"Do I?"

"Of course. Fifteen cents extra."

It turned out she was right.

If you wish to buy socks that are long enough to keep your shinbone from being exposed beneath your trouser cuff, you do not go in and ask the man for long socks. You ask to see some socks in the executive length.

An executive, as far as I know, is a man who executes, who gets things done, and why his socks should be longer than anybody else's—or, for that matter, why he should get a slice of tomato and a fistful of potato chips with his cheeseburger—is more than I can explain on short notice.

I stand with those who hold that the language must be constantly enriched with new meanings for old ones. But I can't see that we are getting enrichment when one word takes over for a dozen or more.

If it hasn't already happened, it is bound to be a matter of a few days until the economy-size soap-chip box will be the executive size and the executive olive replaces the old-fashioned jumbo type.

Calling a long cigarette king-size may not have made much sense, but at least there was an aura of romance and pageantry about it that disappears when we refer to it as an executive cigarette.

Maybe that's what really irritates me about the word. It's so dull.

We deride our teens for calling everything fabulous, and yet fabulous is a word full of wonder and mystery.

Apparently we would prefer it if they would come home from a dance and say that the music was really executive.

We wonder why the aspirations of our young people rise no higher than the mediocre. But how can we blame them when they see, all around them, a grown-up society in which everyone's dream is to be executive?

The success is the man who not only wears executive socks and eats the Executive Cheeseburger, but who flies on an airline's executive flight, spends the night in an executive hotel suite, uses an executive ballpoint pen and drinks an executive martini.

The Captains and the Kings depart, and perhaps it's just as well, but it's rather saddening that the most exciting thing we can find to replace them with is an executive.

Truth in packaging is the aim of a government program, and one that is badly needed. Anyone who has ever bought a large and decorative sack of huckleberry-kumquat popover mix, only to discover that it was less than two-thirds full, will demand that the condition be rectified. Might we not also move along in the direction of truth in political packaging?

Haven't we all, at one time or another, been taken in by the large and imposing candidate, only to find that the contents were very loosely packed indeed?

At least you can shake the box of cereal and get some idea of what is inside. Unfortunately you cannot shake the statesman to see if he rattles.

With all that reading, who has time to cook?

¶ Most men have spent some time in the armed services, where all the food is dumped on the same tray, and this has broken their will to resist the delicious one-dish casserole dinner.

I guess I have been getting the message all wrong. I thought that cooking, along with everything else around the house, was getting easier. When I go into the store I see ready-mixes and brown-and-serves and one-package-jiffy meals, and what is there to it but pop the stuff into the $500 range and hot it up?

Great-grandmaw, on the other hand, had to start with the live, un-disassembled, unfrozen chicken, rhubarb stalk or whatever.

But I was wrong. I think we can agree that the difficulty of anything can be measured by the amount of instruction it requires.

And women today have to have three shelves of books in order to cook.

How is it that back when Great-grandmaw had all that complicated cooking to do she had all her recipes (or receipts, as she preferred to call them) in her head? Oh, she might have a few jotted down—Aunt Sally Fenstermacher's lamb stew or the fruitcake from Mrs. Brown at the church. Basically, though, she cooked off the cuff.

Today's cook, however, has more cookbooks on the shelves

than she has food. All these years when I had thought cooking was getting simpler, it has been growing more complex.

To prepare a meal now may take only 20 minutes' cooking time, but it involves three hours of research in the technical literature. If you want your daughter to be a good cook, rapid reading is more important than home economics.

The cookbooks that are tumbling hourly from the presses are not, of course, just general manuals on how to boil water or grate a nutmeg. They are specialized.

There are the nationality cookbooks. Water doesn't boil the same way in Armenia that it does in Belgium. There are books to tell you how the French cook, and the Dutch and the Chinese and the New Zealanders.

You might think that eventually the cookbook writers would run out of countries, but look at the way new nations are emerging. *Best Recipes from Chad* or *Cooking à la Dahomey* should be available at the bookstores any minute. If we ever quit getting new countries, then there will be recipes from other planets—*Venusian Victuals* or *Martian Menus*.

Other cookbooks are aimed at the particular kind of person who is going to do the cooking. There are cookbooks for brides, for men, for children, for people with large families, small families or no families, for people who hate food, for one-armed cooks, for cooks in a hurry and for cooks with nothing else to do.

I can just about guarantee that if you want a cookbook that is especially directed toward a woman who has been married 17 years, has three children, dusts right-handed but cooks left, is allergic to thyme, needs to lose weight and is fond of Portuguese delicacies, there is just the one for her. If there isn't, go back in a few weeks and somebody will have written one.

Some cookbooks concentrate on where the cooking is going to take place. They tell you how to cook in your back yard, on a boat, in your room without letting your landlady know about it, in a national park (different from in a state park), on a mountain, in a valley. The only place, as far as I know, that they have missed is how to cook in the kitchen, but there may even be something on that.

There are some books which concentrate on cooking with (or without) some particular ingredient. There are fat-free cookbooks and fat-full cookbooks, there are books on cooking with booze and on cooking without salt. There are books on soups and desserts and little things to stick on toothpicks.

Perhaps the latest type of cookbook is the sort that includes other material along with the recipes. Some sprinkle jokes among the instructions. Others contain reproductions of famous paintings, or offer selected prayers and philosophical ruminations. Some give you song lyrics and games to play with the children while motoring.

Then there are the collections of recipes by famous writers, ballplayers, politicians, bank robbers and ulcer sufferers.

Far be it from me to discourage any trend which puts something on the housewife's bookshelf besides a sprouting sweet potato, but I can't understand how Great-grandmaw got along with only her memory and a few notes, the only one of which we could partly decipher seems to call for a brace of bees and a half-tumblerful of gronches. Among other things.

I should have known better than to write anything about cooking, especially if it included anything even remotely resembling a recipe.

You may imagine that I did not hear from women who had looked all through their cookbooks and card files without finding anything listed under gronches. You have a wild imagination.

Still, I will give myself credit for not actually putting in a recipe. This is the thing to do if what you need in your life is angry letters and telephone calls. Especially if it is the recipe for a regional delicacy.

These things, whether they be corndodgers or johnnycakes, are steeped in tradition. They are not only steeped—they are marinated, simmered and deep-fat-fried in tradition. As a consequence, there is no possible way to arrive at a recipe that anybody will accept as correct.

Writers for the public press in New England never stand short for a button-pusher. All they have to do is print a recipe for clam chowder and include a tomato among the ingredients. Then they can go for a three-week vacation, slooping and lobstering along the rockbound coast, merely leaving instructions with their secretaries to publish the indignant letters. When they get home the missives will still be arriving from Marblehead and Taunton and Santa Monica ("My niece has sent me the clipping of your 'recipe,' desecrating the very name of chowder").

Within the green and pellucid shadows of the mint julep lurk the opportunities for an almost unstoppable flow of communications. The true test of a Kentuckian is not that he knows how to make a mint julep, but that he knows that the way you say to make one is wrong.

The Missouri Conservation Commission's magazine recently carried on its back cover a recipe for hush puppies, extracted from a book on outdoor cooking.

As a calculated risk I will repeat it: 2 cups cornmeal, 2 tablespoons flour, 3½ cups boiling water, 1½ teaspoons salt, 1 teaspoon baking powder, 2 tablespoons melted shortening, 2 tablespoons grated onion, 1½ tablespoons black pepper. Add cornmeal and flour to boiling water, mix well and let cool. Add other ingredients and beat well. Drop by the teaspoonful, on a hot well-greased skillet.

This recipe fell upon a number of hot Southerners, who happened to be attending a convention in Missouri. Immediately they started telephoning the Commission to announce that a hush puppy consisted of cornmeal, water and salt. Anything more was a sinful abomination.

The hush puppy, which has made Mr. Webster's third and more permissive unabridged dictionary, gets its name, of course, from the fact that it was intended to be a sort of sop for Cerberus, to keep the dogs quiet while the catfish were frying. The more Spartan of these two recipes, I would guess, might hush a puppy, but the Conservation Commission's version sounds a little tastier for human consumption.

Well, I am not going to get involved in that particular argument. If you are going to fry hush puppies, do it any way that seems natural to you. Anyway, they now come in jars as a cocktail snack and are undoubtedly made in some large and sterile factory in Rahway, New Jersey (a perfectly nice town).

My point is the rather excessive vehemence with which any effort to offer a regional recipe is received. People, apparently, feel these matters deeply. They do not merely disagree. Instead they offer to meet the author (or his proxy) at the border with a welcoming committee and a rope.

I have often been tempted to invent an old family recipe for a completely fictional dish, such as raisin goshawfuls.

Then all I would have to do would be to sit back and wait for the letters and telephone calls informing me that only an obviously idiotic carpetbagger would print a recipe like that.

I can envision a typical letter now: "My sainted grandmother would be turning in her grave if she thought any descendant of hers would ever put raisins in a goshawful."

¶ KNOW THYSELF,

BORING THOUGH IT MAY BE

The trouble with this business is that it can't be kept impersonal. The man whose assignment is to write funny is like the man who has been told off to write poetical; he is bound to get personally involved. The "I" inserts itself in both cases, which nobody cares for, but just about has to be.

The only alternatives are something like "we" or "your reporter." The poet will understand. How would it have done for Richard Lovelace to write, "We would not love thee, dear, so much, loved we not honour more"?

Keats, I think we can all agree, would have lost something had he phrased it, "When your reporter has fears that he may cease to be."

So, from time to time, I find myself writing about myself. This sort of public exposure of the inmost me can, of course, be embarrassing, but at least the self-interview can be conducted in comparative comfort, whereas Walter Lippmann or Scotty Reston and people like that have to be out chasing after their sources in all kinds of weather.

What are cubes to me, or I to them?

Have you ever looked into an empty icebox or (to use the current euphemism) refrigerator? Perhaps you have. I generally find that you are more sophisticated than I am. You have been to drive-in movies and water-skied and read *Doctor Zhivago* and been to Banff and eaten steamed clams.

I lack these experiences and many more which are commonplace to you. So it seems reasonable that you might not share the awe and wonder with which I first looked into an empty icebox.

New experiences are often wasted on the young. Show Old Faithful geyser to a 9-year-old and he asks, "So what else does it do?"

But when you come to these things in your middle years, they have impact.

The late Keats got a tremendous charge out of first looking into Chapman's Homer. He would have understood how I felt on first looking into an empty refrigerator.

I approached it with the same hushed reverence this same Keats paid to a Grecian urn.

Picture that vast cavern, the interior of an Ice-o-Dandy Deluxe—brooding, mysterious. Sir Edmund Hillary, gazing from the pinnacle of Everest into the icy profundities of the crevasses which thereabouts abound, I salute as a fellow initiate into this particular mystery.

Do you know that there are back walls on refrigerators? Of course you do. So do I. I accept it intellectually. But always my view has been blocked by a half-hacked roast, a bowl of macaroni, a forest of salad dressing bottles, a congeries of popsicles.

Toward the rear of the refrigerator, in my experience, is a wasteland, an unexplored area, a terra incognita, where dwell little, squat bowls, plastic-covered, of leftovers long forgotten and bottles turned upside down to catch the final drops of whatever they might contain.

Here, suddenly, was a full, uninterrupted view of the entire interior. No bacon perched precariously upon the bottle of milk, no cheese dips, no unidentifiable objects wrapped in foil, no six-pack of whatever.

I saluted the chasteness of that magic grot with a Keatsian salute.

"Hello, in there," I said, "thou still unravish'd bride of quietness, thou foster-child of silence and slow time!"

I got back, so help me, an echo.

In spite of the evidence, I am not a complete idiot, and I know that refrigerators are brought into this world empty, just as children arrive in mint condition—free from sin (never mind the theology of the matter). But I had never seen one that way.

To confine ourselves to the mechanical era of refrigeration, thus getting rid of all nostalgia involving the horse-drawn ice wagon and the card you put in the window and the man with tongs and the burlap sack on his shoulder who used to kid with Olga, the jewel of a maid, I have looked into many a refrigerator. I knew them when they had their machinery in the basement and when they wore it on top like a hat.

But always they have been full, maybe not of food—there have been tough times, too—but of bottles and cans and jars.

What happened was that, to sustain the economy, we have just made a Major Purchase. This refrigerator is not only new; it is enormous.

After looking into it, after refreshing my soul by its sheer breathtaking emptiness, I was appalled by the suggestion that we put stuff into it. I felt like throwing myself in front of it and crying, "No! Call Secretary Udall. We must preserve the last remaining scrap of virgin wilderness. Sully me not this icy fastness with a tartar sauce jar. Contaminate me not this reminder of undefiled solitariness with a pop bottle. Let's make it a National Park."

To me it was like Glenn and Cooper and the boys getting their first gander into Outer Space—fantastic.

I have not prevailed. The thing is now just as full of the mundane edibles and drinkables of civilization as was its predecessor. It is just another icebox. The poetry, the magic, is gone.

Why do we create these beautiful things, only to desecrate them?

You know what would happen to Great-grandmaw if she had to spend a day around the modern home? She'd be hiding in the closet, that's what. All she had to worry about in her time were packs of wolves and bands of hostile Indians. Otherwise, her peace of mind was pretty much unruffled.

But what happens to Great-granddaughter? She goes through a daily course of lurking figures, war whoops and eerie howls that would have sent Great-grandmaw skedaddling back to Pennsylvania. But, of course, today there is no safety even in Pennsylvania.

There has been the guy who tells her that the house is about to tumble down around her ears on account of the termites, and one who tells her that the furnace is a bomb, just sitting there ticking away, waiting to send her and her near and dear out through the roof.

Speaking of the roof, a passing philanthropist, who just happened to be in this part of the country, has noticed that the roof is about to dissolve in the next rain and stops by to chill her with the information.

The man from the encyclopedia has been around to tell her that her child's brain is in danger of being shrunk down to the size of a pea if the home does not include the entire 148-volume set with the complimentary bookcase in a choice of walnut or pecky cypress finish. And if the child escapes mental stultification, there are even worse things in store unless an attachment goes into the water system to either take something out or put it in.

Outside the house things are just as bad. The trees are dying, the lawn has been poisoned and the driveway is granulating.

Maybe Great-grandmaw was pestered by Indians, but they weren't trying to sell her aluminum awnings or tinted photographs of her children.

¶ A friend has one of those completely automatic kitchens, except for an old-fashioned icebox, the kind that has to be personally defrosted. He says he wants to feel that something around the place *needs* him.

What psychiatrist handled your psyche last?

It's a pretty good bet that when Ug the caveman took his stone hatchet to the naborhood stone-hatchet fix-it man to be sharpened, the friendly fix-it man said, "Hey, Mac, who's been sharpening this thing? They sure made a mess of it."

The most amazing thing about Delilah is that she did not remark to Samson, "Honey, I hate to say it, but whoever trimmed you last was a real hacker."

Or maybe she did, because this impulse of the craftsman to take a jaundiced view of whatever colleague preceded him on the job seems to be universal.

A classic example involves the veteran baseball player who was sent out to right field to replace an inept rookie. After an inning in which he had dropped two pop flies, he reported to the manager, "That kid had right field so loused up nobody could play it."

(There are many versions of this anecdote; one is no better than another.)

A general's memoirs make it clear that his first task, upon taking over the command, was to straighten out the horrible botch his predecessor had made of things.

In political circles it is known as "inheriting the situation." It enables any national administration to get through most of its first term by blaming everything that goes wrong on the crowd that was in charge during the four years just past.

We doff our hats in tribute to the vaudeville performer who, when asked how the audience received him, replies, "Who knows? They were still booing the act ahead of mine."

("That song-and-dance team has the stage so loused up nobody can play it.")

In the case of most artisans I don't think there is anything unkind about their denigrating the men who did the work before them. I think it is pretty much an ordinary conversation-opener. It is meant mainly to put the customer, patient, or client at ease.

When you're fixing a man's guttering, it helps to tell him that the last man who fixed his gutters didn't know his elbow from his overflow. It cheers him with the feeling that, at long last, his guttering is in good hands.

I remember an eye doctor who asked me, "Who looked into your eyes like this last?"

"Kim Novak," I replied. He added the witticism to my bill.

What I want to suggest is that those of us who are not particularly expert at anything should be allowed to get in on this thing.

I don't mind the garageman asking who ground those valves last, the shoeman inquiring as to who made such a disaster of my shoes or the income tax man shaking his head over who made out my return in 1960.

But I want a piece of the action.

There probably isn't any way I can do it in my line of work, so it will have to be done around the house.

Next time I miss the nail and mash my thumb: "O.K., who used this hammer last?"

While tying a bow in my little girl's sash: "Honey, would you mind telling me who tied this sash last?"

At homework time: "Somebody's got this algebra so mixed up nobody can work it."

I am timid about swimming pools. Not from fear of drowning. Once I'm in the water I'm O.K. But I remember a few years ago one of our popular idols—Frank Sinatra or some such —received a nasty wound when he stepped on a martini toothpick at the edge of a swimming pool. Whenever I walk around a pool I peer intently at the ground to be sure there are no toothpicks lying there.

I am taking no chances.

I don't want to have to go to my doctor and explain to him that I stepped on a toothpick from somebody's martini at the edge of a swimming pool. Doctors tend to think that anything that happens to me is funny enough as it is.

¶ Elementary History is the study of what our ancestors did. Advanced History is the study of why they shouldn't have.

Alone and unarmed among editorial writers

¶ Man prides himself on being the only thinking animal, and yet thinking is the one excuse for inactivity that no wife or employer will accept.

I moved my desk the other day, which was the most interesting thing that has happened to me lately, and if you think that it doesn't interest anybody else, I want to tell you that you're wrong.

The minute the desk was put in place, clean across the room, after sixteen years in one location, there was darkness at noon. The lights went out. Rain fell as though some cosmic conventioneer had dropped a huge water bomb upon the city. Ducks drowned, tornado funnels were sighted.

Somebody, apparently, was interested. I say no more.

Although the old neighborhood was comfortable, the new situation has advantages for a Beginning Thinker that are almost unbelievable. I am between the farm editor and the international affairs editor. The desk on my southern border is littered with foreign newspapers and press releases from countries that I didn't even know had governments, much less mimeograph machines.

The desk adjoining me to the north is the recipient of the full fallout of the press machinery of the Department of Agriculture and nonpolitical brochures on the insects of Kansas.

It is, as you can imagine, a stimulating place to be at this moment in history. To my right, the great world, with its global problems, the clash of armies, the maneuverings of diplomats. To my left, the grass roots, the soil, water and climate, a feel for the real concern of everyday folks.

I feel that I am a part of two worlds—a connecting link between bib overalls and striped pants. A heavy obligation.

Where I am is in the middle of the editorial writers, and it gives a man an eerie feeling to think that he is surrounded by continual cogitation.

You are sitting there straightening out a paper clip and endeavoring to keep the mind blank and supple in case an idea should wander by, and it brings you up short when you find an editorial writer looking at you.

You start to smile and wave your paper clip, and then you realize he is not looking at you, he is looking through you.

"That man, I do believe," you say to yourself, "is thinking."

Have you ever watched a man think? It is an unnerving experience and drives you (or me) to the water cooler. (From which, incidentally, I am now separated by—in addition to editorial writers—the assistant Sunday editor, the Sunday editor, the city editor, three of those machines that click all day long and a desk where a pleasant gentleman has worked every day for years without revealing to me—or possibly to anyone else— exactly what it is he does. He may be in charge of desk moving.)

Cerebrating, in case you haven't seen any lately, is a very visual thing. Little balloons appear over the heads of the thinkers, and in one it says "Algeria" and in another "Outer Space" and in another "The Budget" and so on, according to what this particular fellow is thinking about.

The first day in the new location I sent up some balloons that caused a lot of angry looks from the editorial writers, and when I looked up and saw what was in them I understood why, and hurriedly pulled them down and stuffed them into the bottom right-hand drawer of my desk, where I peek in at them from time to time.

Right now I have a balloon which has nothing in it but a log and a saw and a lot of zzzzz's. The feeling is that it isn't the sort of balloon that adds much to the intellectual atmosphere, but at least it keeps people from disturbing me.

The press and so on are always picking on us middle-agers. Like you read in the paper a great big banner headline which says MIDDLE-AGED HUBBY ELOPES WITH BABY-SITTER. Or you pick up a magazine and there is an article about how most embezzlers are middle-aged.

It is disappointing to us middle-agers that nobody writes about the vast majority of us who never elope with baby-sitters and do not embezzle and are always stopping and helping old ladies change their flat tires.

There is all sorts of stuff in the public media about what a mess we middle-agers are physically. We are too fat, it says in one write-up; we are bald, it says elsewhere; and still another smart aleck says we do not go to our doctors often enough and are all about to have heart attacks.

How do you think this makes the middle-ager feel?

I know a number of middle-aged boys and girls and they are as fine and clean-cut a group as you would ever want to meet. Do these people who are always saying superciliously, "Oh, well, what can you expect? He is a middle-ager," when one of us has made a little mistake, really know any middle-agers? Have they ever had them into their homes or baked them some cookies or just talked to them? I'll bet not.

Take a look around your neighborhood. There is a Teen-Town for the youngsters and a Golden Age Club for the old people. But does anybody care about the middle-ager?

No. There is nothing for them to do. It's no wonder that some of them—a minority, true, but still too many—are robbing banks and smoking cigars.

People are quick to condemn the middle-ager and they forget that they either were that age once themselves or someday will be.

Let's try to leave the kind of world the bugs will appreciate

I had been apprehensive that recent public attention to cockroaches might bring word from Archie, the cockroach who used to write notes to Don Marquis by hurling himself from the top of the typewriter onto the keys below. Sure enough, the following manuscript was found in my typewriter the other morning:

to whom it may concern
there has not been a good columnist
in america
since don marquis died
which is why i have been living in
retirement at a restaurant which
i will not not give you the address of
as it is one of the last
real oases
of continental sanitation
that has not succumbed to the
current craze for cleanliness.
if i told you where it was then
it would be ruined by the tourist
trade,
little cockroaches in berets
and with their wives and
kids,
i shudder
to think of it.
i hate to say this,
having been an ink-stained
wretch,
as alex woollcott put it,
in my time,
but even newspaper offices
are becoming disgustingly
clean, ugh.
on the old sun when i
worked for don marquis
there was always a
sandwich lying around.
not much to feed the soul
of a transmogrified
vers libre poet but it
served
for a cockroach.

now
what do i see but
all the food in vending
machines and not even
a crumb anywhere
or if there is a cafeteria
it is immaculate and
enough to make you
sick.
the reason that i am
coming out of retirement
at this time is that
the scientists say that
we cockroaches stand to
inherit
the earth
in case of the bomb.
i wish i could work
the shift lever but i
suppose you realize that when
i say
the bomb
i mean
the upper case
bomb.
we can absorb more radiation
than anybody else.
what i want to say is that
we cockroaches appreciate
it, but we really dont
want to be the only people
around.
i dont want to be a traitor
to my class but ive been
around cockroaches a lot
and theyre no better than people.
so what i want to do

is tell
everybody that we cockroaches
are in no hurry.
wed just as soon not have
the world on our shoulders
even if we had shoulders.
the least you can do
in return is dirty
up the restaurants a little bit
and you might leave a half
a sandwich around like
don marquis used to
do.
on pumpernickel.
thank you.
                    archie.

¶ "It takes a colony of termites 30 years to undermine the average frame house." This is also the length of the GI mortgage. You make the last payment on the day the place collapses.

"They keep telling us," he said, "that what the country needs is fewer spectators and more participants. But take a football game. For a spectator, there is the matter of parking two miles from the stadium, with the resultant walk requiring the climbing and descent of historic Old Main hill, the ascent to the top of the stadium, the squirming through a hard-nosed phalanx of other spectators to one's seat, the trip to the coffee counter between halves and the ugly scenes of physical contact which there occur.

"Looking on it objectively, and with due respect to our leaders, it seems to me that we spectators get a tremendous amount of exercise in a football afternoon."

"But the players—" I said.

"Time-study engineers," he answered, "have shown that the average football participant spends some five minutes in actual play during a game—a figure which I think you will concede is ridiculous compared with the physical energy dissipated by a spectator.

"As far as baseball is concerned, a leading sportswriter and I have figured out that five minutes would about cover the time an outfielder spends in exerting himself during a nine-inning game, even if he gets a hit and including running to and from his position. I personally have spent more time than that trying to flag down a peanut salesman."

"What, then," I asked, "is your suggestion for curing our national flab?"

"Get the young people off the playing field," he said, "and up into the stands where a man has to be tough to survive."

Please, Mr. Motorist, put me back

Terrible amounts are written about the danger of picking up hitchhikers. You have read all about it. The nice young man produces the pistol and you are left beside the highway without pocket watch, money or automobile. You are lucky you have not been hit on the head.

He seemed like such a splendid young fellow, too. His prison uniform was neat, except for a few places where the brick dust had worn off as he went over the wall.

Nobody ever writes about the perils to the hitchhiker. Or not hitchhiker, exactly. Rather, let us say, the man who is waiting for the bus. You have your copy of Herodotus in the original whatever that you intend to read on the slow ride to work. You can't read at home—what with the wife after you to measure the curtains, and the children and the teevy to deal with.

The bus ride stretches ahead as an oasis in the day—a chance to read, to think—perhaps to scheme.

Then the horn honks and the green station wagon stops, and the morning peace is shattered. You are not in too great shape.

Nothing bad, a little fat around the heart or whatever it is that produced the funny look in the doctor's eye when he told you to remember that, after all, at your age . . .

But you spring toward the station wagon, which has overshot you by 150 feet. Conscious of the neighbors watching, you keep the knees high, elbows tucked in.

The way they build cars nowadays, you have to hunker down so you can see the driver and he can see you. This can be kind of painful—the way they build hunkers nowadays.

The Samaritan gets a look at you and you are not the prospective client he thought you were, but he says grudgingly, "Get in."

So you do, trying to hide the Herodotus under your coat.

Waves of silence waft you toward downtown. With horror you watch the driver taking turn after turn that leads you farther from where you want to go. But what can you say? You are a guest. His Hydro-jet-oramatic is his castle.

"Where you goan?" he finally inquires graciously.

"Never mind," you say, "it's been such a big, tremendous, unforgettable help, just let me out wherever you can get off this turnpike before we get to Seattle, you idiot."

Eventually you get out at First Avenue and Ploughed Ground, within a leisurely 45-minute stroll of your desk.

Or, even worse, it is someone you know, or almost know. For block after block, past filling stations and veterinarians' and guitar studios and boardinghouses and bars and haberdasheries and drive-ins and vacant lots you both grapple with the problem of what to say to each other.

You are each equally unsure of the other's name, but too sure that you are supposed to know each other to reach over and announce, with a hearty handshake, "Nitnot is the name."

It makes for a long ride—and, without Herodotus, a lonely one.

You can also get picked up by people who want to impeach Earl Warren, recognize Red China, ban the bomb, repeal the income tax or tell you how much mileage they get out of this car and what the trade-in was on the old one.

I do not mention any of these things in a spirit of carping criticism. But merely to point out that the hazards of the road apply to the passenger as well as to the driver.

¶ Today the Good Samaritan would be sued for moving the poor soul before the insurance adjuster got there.

Among the many reasons the country has for being thankful that I am not its President is that I do not have the type of memorabilia a President should have to spruce up the executive office.

In the first place you have to have some historic prints, preferably of ships, to hang on the walls. Most of our recent Presidents have been very heavy in this department, but outside of a snapshot of some idiot from Cleveland I met in Minnesota one time, standing up in a rowboat and holding a clutch of walleyes, I can't produce any waterborn art. The name on the boat is the Daisy IV. The name of the idiot I can't remember, but he not only repeated the punch lines of all his jokes, but in between repetitions he asked, "Ya sure you didn't hear it before?" What kind of a country would it be with a picture of an idiot like that on the White House wall, in or out of a boat?

The only historic print I have is very big and handsome and has been my favorite work of art since early boyhood. It shows scalpings and pistols with little puffs of smoke coming out of them, and the title underneath is "Custer's Last Fight."

There is also, underneath it, a commercial for a brewery.

Boy, I can just see the First Lady, any First Lady, letting me hang that historic print right behind the President's desk. I like it; it relaxes me. And I would put up something of a struggle for it, I suppose.

There are a lot of times, I imagine, when the President must feel like Custer, with the hostiles of Congress and the Kremlin and the press moving in on him. It might do him good to be able to look there on the wall and see old Custer taking it with equanimity.

Of course, Custer didn't come out of it so good, but that very fact might be a warning to a President to have a little humility and not get too carried away unless he knew the territory.

I can remember stuff I never even heard of

¶ Even the skeptic must admit that there may be something in prenatal memories when the kid sportswriter writes his recollections of Napoleon Lajoie.

¶ Grandfather can't understand how the kids can do their homework with television. And they can't imagine how he could have done his without the telephone.

For some reason there seems to be more nostalgia in my set than there was, say, 25 years ago.

People sit around and they say, "Boy, do you remember licorice whips and those little sugar hearts with mottoes on them and sleeve garters?"

And somebody else says, "Boy, I sure remember the bejabers out of those items you mention, and also fifteen-cent Rocket baseballs and John Bunny and 'The Bungles' and climbing up on the back step of the ice wagon."

And everybody starts remembering the Chalmers and the Apperson Jack-Rabbit and Eppa Jephtha Rixie and J. Ham Lewis and how good homemade peach ice cream tasted when you got to lick the paddle as a reward for turning the crank.

And people remember long underwear and McGuffey's Readers and Irving Aaronson and his Commanders and cat-whisker radios and mumblety-peg.

Well, some of this stuff I remember and some I don't. I remember throwing a golf ball against the concrete steps and every time you caught it, why, that was a man on base, and if it hit the edge of the step that was a home run and—but it was pretty complicated; I'd have to show you.

But I lack the total recall that other people have.

Or seem to have. Do they really remember all those things? Nobody ever says they don't remember something. Not even women will admit it, even though the remembering makes them about 20 years older than they are.

When it comes to nostalgia, the great American pride in being young seems to break down. Everybody wants to say they remember home brew and celluloid collars, *Tom Swift* and Milton Sills.

Lately I have started testing my theory that people don't really remember the things they say they do.

I'll say something like "Boy, do you remember how swell it used to feel early in the morning when you'd go out in your bare feet and walk on the barbed wire and smell the new-mown string beans?"

And everybody says that yes, yes, they remember that very well and rush on to a memory of their own.

Or I will say, "Hey, do you remember those octagonal pink penny candies that were full of strychnine?" and they will clap their hands and say indeed, indeed, they remember them well.

I will ask, "Do you remember when we used to wear yellow slickers with crazy jokes written on them and dance the minuet?"

"Do you remember the fireworks when General Benedict Arnold came to town?"

"Do you remember the early days of radio with Mozart beating out his own stuff on the 88?"

"Do you remember when hand-knit carburetors were all the rage and all the girls wore porte-cocheres?"

"Boy, how about, boy, the time they let out school when Walter Damrosch hit 63 home runs?"

"Do you remember when no home was complete without an Isotta-Fraschini in the front parlor and no nice girl spoke English?"

Yes, yes, indeed, indeed, everybody cries, and they are not even interrupted in their outpouring of rememberings about peekaboo blouses and horse cars and the St. Louis Browns.

In fact, at the end of an evening, they often seek me out to say they don't see how I can remember all those things which they might almost have forgotten if I hadn't reminded them.

She called me typical, but she smiled

Boy, some of the dumb things they give these kids their Ph.D. for these days. It makes you wonder what kind of education they think they're turning out in these dopey universities.

Like here is a girl, one of these coeds out at Southern Cal who does this thesis on what is a typical newspaperman like, and she says, for one thing, he is emotionally unstable and excitable.

If I was emotionally unstable or excitable I wouldn't be sitting here, chewing on this swizzle stick, would I? No, I'd go out to Southern Cal and maybe blow the place up or give the prexy at least a knuckle sandwich. What a dumb thesis!

Listen to this where this girl, talking about us average newspapermen, says, "He is particularly irresponsible when it comes to money." That's a laugh. Ask anybody. Ask my wife. I lose a week's pay playing poker, why, I worry about it. When I get home I wake up my wife and tell her how worried I am about losing the week's pay playing poker, know what I mean? Isn't that about as responsible as a man can get, worrying all the time like that?

In fact, I finally got so responsible about money that the wife now comes down and collects the pay herself. She's afraid that all this responsibility I got is going to end me up worried sick or something.

You haven't got ten bucks that isn't working for you that you could lend me the use of until Tuesday, have you? I got word of something going in the third at Hialeah.

No? That's all right. And it proves how wrong this thesis writer is on another point.

She says, right here, the typical newspaperman is "pessimistic and broods about himself."

Am I brooding about you not giving me the use of the ten?

Of course not. I am maybe reminding myself of the time when a certain party not three feet from me at this very moment was in the hospital, and who was it came out to see him a couple of times and brought him a basket of fruit and asked him if he needed any dough he'd go on his note?

I'm reminding myself about that and a lot of other stuff when a certain party was all full of gratitude, and I'm telling myself that you finally find out what your friends are like when you ask them for a miserable ten only just until Tuesday, but I'm not brooding about it.

And on the pessimistic thing, why, that's wrong, too. I was optimistic all along. I was hoping you wouldn't give me the ten because if you did the horse would lose. All my horses always lose. I know they're going to lose, so where does this kid get that pessimistic jazz?

This girl is quoted in *Newsweek* magazine and it's hard to find anything that she's got right. For instance, she says we typicals come from "an unhealthy emotional climate." Where does she get that? I was screaming at my kids just this morning that if they didn't shape up and show a little more appreciation of this healthy emotional climate I'm breaking my back to give them, I'd crack their necks.

And she says we make impulsive decisions. Somebody must have told her about the time I went down to the dock to see Ed What-was-his-name—the little guy who always wore the bow ties—off for Europe.

And there was all that trouble with the steamship line about me not having any ticket or anything and the State Department was sore about the passport, and the smallpox thing was kind of a mess. Now, I put it to you that an impulsive man would have thought twice before stirring up all that trouble for himself, now, wouldn't he?

There wasn't anything impulsive about it. I'd been thinking about going to Europe for 30 years. Off and on.

Get this where she says, "He is sociable with close friends and sexually aggressive toward women." How about that for a couple of howls? I'm being sociable with you, right? And I don't necessarily regard you as a particularly close friend, except maybe close with a ten-spot. That's about as close a friend as you are.

Sexually aggressive? See that blonde over there at the next table? Have I made a move? Have I done one single thing except maybe wink a couple of times? You call a wink aggressive? Maybe that blond dish there thinks a wink is aggressive. I think maybe I'll just slide over and see what her opinion might just happen to be.

Now that I've filled you in on that nutty Ph.D.

It was a real pleasure to put your book down

¶ "What do you mean I don't write with compassion?" a distinguished author demanded at a recent literary reception. "Anybody says I don't write with compassion gets a punch in the nose."

Many and many a friend has said to me that when I am in New York I should not attempt the literary cocktail party.

"They will spring things on you like participles and James Joyce and the new criticism and you will be regarded as a boob," many and many have said.

I will admit the idea was frightening before I went to my first literary cocktail party. I was afraid that I would drop the name of a favorite author, like Burt L. Standish, and it would turn out that he was an out author and I should have said Dame Edith Sitwell.

But I learned that you can mention Burt L. Standish or Dame Edith Sitwell or Julia Moore, the Sweet Singer of Michigan, and you will find it doesn't make any difference, because every author is only interested in one author, namely, himself.

I had thought that when I met an author I should ask him something pertinent to the craft, such as "Parm me, sir, but what is your *Weltanschauung* on the human continuum?"

But the authors I have met at these things want to talk only about their tax situation and what's wrong with their publishers.

According to the best literary minds of mid-century the problems that are challenging mankind today are expressed in remarks such as these:

"I sent my wife into every bookstore within ten blocks of Times Square to ask for the book, and none of them ever heard of the book."

"You call this guy a tax expert? He couldn't get a capital gains deal for Bill Shakespeare."

"So I told them. I said you put a green cover on the book and it's dead. I was having lunch with this alleged editor and I called the waiter over and I said, 'You ever buy a book with a green cover?' And he said no. So what happens? They put a green cover on it and it just lies there on the shelves. They say it's a bad time of year or the economic situation. It's that green cover."

"Look, I got this great little tax guy and he works out a great setup. The only thing is I got to live in Spain. With my ulcers, I should live in Spain? This is the kind of great little tax guy I got."

The only trouble here is that I know as little about the more rarefied tax problems and the more horrifying things that are wrong with publishers as I do about Virginia Woolf or the private life of J. D. Salinger.

So, at the first couple of literary cocktail parties I attended, I was largely silent—an intolerable state of affairs. The other evening, however, I discovered what to say. I was in a group with two writers whose books had just been published. I was not familiar with their work, nor with their problems with their so-and-so tax men or their this-and-that publishers.

Inspiration arrived.

"How many pages you got in your books?" I asked. Fate for once was playing along with me. One of them had 176 pages. The other one had 214.

"I got," I said, spearing an anchovy, which isn't on my diet, "284 pages in my book."

Well, after that I was the lion of the occasion, and their des-
perate attempts to reintroduce their exorbitant taxes and their
idiotic publishers fell flat.

As a final, and perhaps unjustifiable, touch upon leaving, I
said heartily, "Good luck with your little books."

¶ "Man has no wishbone." And how dull this must
make the big family dinner for the cannibal child.

One thing about snobbishness, it keeps you young

¶ Middle age is when the family stops giving you
neckties for your birthday, figuring that you have enough to last.

¶ Middle age is when you start losing interest in little
filler items that begin "Middle age is when . . ."

A snob I have never been. Uttering my barbaric yawp, I
scorn classification, stratification. What is social class to me or
me to it? I am myself democratic, one with the sailor lonely on
the mizzenpeak, the farmer at his chores, the shopkeeper at his
accounts.

Up until now, that is. Now I have joined a class. It's the only
thing I have ever belonged to. I want it in my obituary.

I am upper-middle-class. Tough on the other classes, but it's
sort of like rush week on the campus. You have to pick out the
group that seems to suit you best.

There are some ways, I'll admit before somebody else brings
them up, where I don't fit the upper-middle-class patterns.
They are minor matters like not making much money and only
having one automobile and no boat to tow behind even that.

I don't belong to a country club, carry a credit card, drink
Scotch, take color slides, ski, deduct my lunches from my in-

come tax or wear neckties made by royalty. I have never been to one of those places where people go in the winter to wear shorts and ride bicycles.

I still think golf is played with mashies and niblicks—that's what it says on my clubs. The thing we play records on I call a Victrola and it only has one speaker.

I don't know any politicians, actors or headwaiters by their first names and would just as soon keep it that way.

In the army of life I am, as I was in the Army of the United States, an enlisted man, and proud to be and have been.

The thing that attracts me to the upper-middle class is not any thought of pomp or glory. It's just that middle age starts later there.

I have been reading a report from the University of Chicago (which is the place to get reports, if you want a friendly tip) which says that upper-middle-class men believe that middle age starts at 47. This is the best offer you can get. In the lower-middle-class it's 45, while in the upper-lower and lower-lower it's 40.

You may object that this is only what the men interviewed think about things. Merely because an upper-middle-class man (my bunch) thinks middle age starts at 47, while others put it younger, doesn't mean there is really any difference.

Well, I'll tell you that it's what a man thinks that counts. And if we—my class, that is—get together and agree that middle age begins at 47 and anybody who gets middle-aged before then can't come to the spring prom, why, then that's it.

In my own case this is like a reprieve. A while back I read that middle age officially began at 45. It made me feel terrible. But it obviously wasn't a University of Chicago report. Furthermore, whoever made the survey was hanging around with a gang of lower-middles and who knows what all. But I fell for it.

Now the load has been lifted. With middle age postponed until 47, I have seven months of youth left. It's like finding some change behind the sofa cushions, a forgotten cigar in the pocket of your other suit.

If it means moving up to upper-middle I accept the challenge.

In fact, I'd even take a try at lower-upper or upper-upper. The chances are that in those classes middle age doesn't arrive until you're maybe 70.

In fact, the only millionaire I ever knew fairly well was called Junior in his sixties.

What makes me feel old is nothing internal or some child star getting arrested for giving marijuana to his grandchildren. What does it for me is the major league baseball players who blow gum bubbles.

Here's the thing: Most of us grow up secure in the knowledge that major league baseball players are older than we are. How could they be anything else? They are big fellows and chew tobacco and if they notice us outside the park they say, "Hello, kid."

Intellectually, with the old skull, I know that those men out there on the diamond, awesome though they may appear, are about the age of somebody's youngest sister's middle boy. But I never think about it, under ordinary circumstances. When they are performing they are ageless. The rawest rookie, standing in at the plate, looks about the same age as Ty Cobb used to.

Until they blow the bubble.

There goes the illusion. Suddenly they are their actual age, and a chilling wind blows in from left field reminding me that time passes and that the league's leading slugger may very well have worn a beanie with a propeller on top.

No reason why he shouldn't have. No reason why he shouldn't chew bubble gum. But the twinge, old pal, is there.

My last exclusive . . .

One trouble with my dreams is that I always seem to have the same personal and professional shortcomings in them that I do in real life. Other men, from what I hear, dream about exotic places, with native charmers and great, green breakers bashing the coral strands and this is all very pleasant and they lie there with a smile which alarms their wives.

Well, my problem is that when I dream about some far-off place like that I can never enjoy it because the hotel in the dream won't cash a check and I am running out of money. This, as you may guess, is no relief at all from being awake.

The other night I had a dream in which I was given an assignment to interview an actor named Richard Burton.

The next morning I told my wife about it and she wanted to know what I asked him, and I said that I had asked him where he was born.

"Pontrhydyfen, South Wales," he had replied.

My wife said that nobody had dreams in which people said they were born in Pontrhydyfen, South Wales, even if they were, which, as I later found out, is true in Richard Burton's case.

"He said he was born Richard Jenkins in Pontrhydyfen, South Wales, on November 10, 1925," I continued. "It was all very vivid in the dream. And then he wanted to know if there was anything else I wanted to ask him."

Well, I said to my wife, I told him I couldn't think of anything.

"You don't have much of a story, do you?" he said.

"No," I had to admit, "but I really don't know what else would be interesting. Unless you have something to suggest."

He said he hadn't, but gave me a publicity handout with the names of all the movies he had been in. I thanked him and copied them down and told him I hadn't actually seen any of them but for him not to feel too bad about it because I don't go to a great many movies.

He said he wouldn't.

And I said that I bet if I had seen any of them I would have thought they were swell.

He thanked me.

I looked over my notes, and I had to admit again that the story didn't have a whole lot of zing to it, so I asked him what he had been doing lately.

He said he had been over in Rome, and I asked him if he had eaten at any of the places where an aunt of mine ate once when she was on a tour with a group of other schoolteachers. He pretended that he had.

Then I thought of a real good idea and asked him if he would rather act in the movies or on the stage. He said that they were quite different and I said that I supposed that was true.

He went on to add that on the stage the actor has more of a sense of being in touch, so to speak, with the audience than he does on the screen. I made him repeat that so I could copy it down.

I told him that I guessed that just about covered everything and he said was I sure and I said yep, and put my notebook in my pocket and that was the end of the interview.

My wife looked at me.

"And that was all you asked Richard Burton?" she inquired.

"In the dream, yes," I said. "In real life I suppose I would have asked him what he thought of the New York Mets and nuclear testing and the skyline and so on, to get a few more newsy quotes. What do you want me to do? Ask him some cornball cliché like what does he think of American women?"

Well, she told me some things I should have asked him. As I say, I don't seem to do any better in my dreams than I do during the day.

Some of the questions my wife suggested were very interesting.

A man has to keep his bubble vulcanized

Speaking at a convention of architects, Dr. Edward T. Hall, an anthropologist, introduced me, if not his other listeners, to the idea of the space bubble.

As I understand it, the idea is that we all move about in an invisible sack of personal space, and when anybody (except, presumably, a loved one) gets close enough to impinge upon our bubble, we are uncomfortable if not irate.

Being an anthropologist, accustomed to taking broad views, Dr. Hall emphasizes that the size of the space bubbles varies among nationalities. The Japanese, for example, are perfectly happy with about a size 5 space bubble, which the American would find extremely chafing. And it's not only because the Japanese are smaller; it's that they can maintain their sense of personal privacy even when things get pretty crowded.

At the other extreme, I suppose, is the American of pioneer days who felt that two smudges of smoke on the horizon meant that his bubble was being invaded and it was time to move on.

I know nothing about these national differences in the size of the space bubble, but I have noticed some interesting variations among individuals here in this country.

Perhaps we no longer have people with space bubbles the size of the pioneer's, which stretched from horizon to horizon. But there still are people walking around in pretty-good-sized bubbles.

Engraved on memory's tablet is a lady with a big bubble who lived in our neighborhood when I was young. Every time I as much as set foot on the vacant lot next to the apartment where she lived (on the third floor), she would scream, "Get away from here, you nasty little boy."

(I will not stoop to mention that, though I was undeniably little, I was never nasty.)

At the time I thought she was merely overly sensitive. Now I realize that she could not help it; she was a prisoner inside an oversized space bubble.

For some reason the tightest-fitting space bubbles I have encountered have been those surrounding politicians. Here, again, they differ, but there is no denying that most of our elected leaders like to work in close.

The politician with a small bubble doesn't care how big your own personal bubble may be. He is clutching your lapel, stabbing your sternum with his forefinger, slapping you on the back, twisting your elbow while he shakes your hand.

After an encounter with a small-bubble politician it may take hours to get your punctured bubble repaired with all the leaks vulcanized.

Democracy is, of course, worth any price, and the wear and tear on one's bubble is slight. Monarchs always traveled in tremendous bubbles. Nobody could get close, and this often infuriated people, who chopped off the heads of kings because their bubbles were so big.

Dictators, too, have big bubbles, with bodyguards on the outside to keep folks away.

Anyway, to me it is a charming picture: Each of us inside his own little capsule of private space. And even in the case of the individual it must vary from time to time. You had better, for example, wear a much smaller bubble to a crowded cocktail party than when you are out shooting pheasant.

I am so intrigued by the whole idea that next time I am on a department store elevator I am going to turn around and say, "Lady, your umbrella is impinging upon my space bubble."

I suppose someday they'll have automatic elevators to the point where they'll scan you with an electric eye and put together a few facts, such as the color of your necktie and the crease in your pants, and decide you are Mr. Ephemeral from ninth floor, and that's where you'll end up, no matter who you are.

I'm not even sure that automatic elevators don't recognize people now. At least they seem to know me, judging by the way they are always trying to catch me in their doors.

¶ British housewives, according to a recent study, put a new refrigerator at the head of their list of things they wanted most. This is remembered as the survey with the fridge on top.

Gungwuk Simmons is three generations away from Venus, but the way he acts you'd think he was just off the rocket.

Frankly, it's kind of a pain in the neck; you go over to his house and there's nothing on the hi-fi but "Groncho Larp" and "Orch ne 1Lo?" and everything cooked with algae, which is O.K., but can get to be a little much—like, I mean, in the ice cream?

My old man gets a big kick out of Gungwuk. As you know, my old man is from Mars, born on the old planet and, as he says, never breathed oxygen or weighed more than 18 pounds until he came to Earth as a young man.

But he says this is home now and nothing amuses him as much as a professional planetarian like Gungwuk Simmons.

Now, I'll have to admit that when there's something on the teevy like maybe a bunch of Martian folk dancers doing the 3897 and playing on the 6332, or even the tenor 807, he gets a little sentimental, especially if he has had a drink or two of 003, and I've heard him whisper, "7," which was his pet name for my mother. But other than that he never talks Martian.

When old friends come over he says, "No numbers. Speak words. You want to speak numbers go back to Mars and work in the 402 mines." And they all laugh.

My father says there are people who paint themselves red every Mars Day who've never been within a million light years of the place.

Gungwuk Simmons is just the opposite of my father. His wife Nancy says he wears a k, tCH around the house and would wear it to work if she didn't put her foot down.

I dread it when Gungwuk calls me just before lunch because I know he has heard about another place down in Little Venus where you can get the only genuine Venusian cooking in town.

Windows or science: which?

All right, we all know that we are in a bumper-to-bumper race with The Other Guys to see which of us can turn out the most scientists. Every mail brings an appeal for money from some college that you may have passed in the vicinity of. And the taxes are going to have to go up to buy more Bunsen burners for one and all in the State U.

What worries me is that there is not enough emphasis on making sure that the new buildings on our campi don't have windows. I refer particularly to the science buildings.

A window or two in the liberal arts facilities would probably do no harm. The student of English literature may even be assisted by the opportunity to look out at daffodil, skylark, crannied wall (flower in) and other certified conceits.

But it is murder on science.

In my own case, windows blasted a career that would surely have put me right up there with the giants of test tube and cyclotron. I would be wearing a white coat and giving contradictory interviews to the press on the subject of whether fallout is a good thing. I would be signing petitions and attending expense-paid symposia in Scandinavian countries, with maybe sabbatical years and an exchange professorship at Heidelberg.

Great Scott, what a scientist I would have made! I could speak condescendingly of the lay mind. The White House Workshop on Big Ideas would feel the full weight of my elephantine yet impish wit and inhale the aroma of my pungent pipe. *Time* would feature my portrait upon its cover—and not by one of its staff artists who make you look like yourself, but by one of the commissioned geniuses who immortalize the really big faces in green blobs. I would be revealed in newspaper and magazine as crotchety yet lovable, brilliant but down-to-earth, an equal fan of the quantum theory and the New York Mets. I would be esoteric, irascible, absent-minded and, taken all in all, sweet.

Windows did me in.

I had advanced as far as second-year chemistry, which was qualitative and quantitative analysis. I shone, I twinkled. I was the talk of the lab with my inspired guesses plus a good deal of cheating.

The theory of this course, as I understood it, was to find out what was in a lot of little bottles. I had it clearly in mind that lithium burned with a green flame, and everything I tested seemed to burn with a green flame and I put down lithium and it was, fortunately, a big year for lithium, so I was doing well.

Until spring came. And I discovered the windows in the classrooms, especially the laboratories. I can't imagine what architectural idiot built a chemistry laboratory with windows. You could look out of them.

And what you saw was grass and birds and flowers and girls. I didn't want to analyze them. I didn't want to check for chlorophyll and potash and phosphorus and—for all I know—lithium, the things that grass and birds and flowers and—for all I know—girls are made out of.

I just wanted to join them.

So I debarked or decamped or de-labbed. I left. I opted for the grass and birds and flowers and girls.

Those I left behind me, grimly burning lithium, are now members of the new aristocracy of enzymes and chain reactions and mystery ingredients. They were strong enough to resist the lure of the windows. I wasn't.

My plea is that among the students of today there may be others with futures as bright as mine then seemed—men ready to grasp the oyster of unsearchable truth and extract from it the pearl of infinite wisdom, but men also, like me, unable to keep their eyes away from the windows.

Educators of America, with windows in the laboratories I don't know how you ever get your young chemists and physicists through the spring months. Build no more windows, is my advice, and brick up the ones you have.

A man can accomplish many things in his lifetime, but some little facet of his career sticks in the public mind and he's typed forever. It doesn't have to be anything he's particularly proud of. It may be some small error, like running the wrong way in football or failing to touch second base or taking the day's receipts home with him from the store.

That's all anybody wants to talk about when they meet this man. Chances are he would about a hundred times rather change the subject.

Or like once in his life a man mistakes the dog food in the icebox for the leftover hash. For the next thirty years his friends are going "Bowwow" at him, or if he encounters strangers his wife says, "Sam, tell the Hendersons about, you know, the time with the dog food . . ."

Wives don't say, "Sam, tell the Hendersons about the time you rescued the little boy from drowning, or would have if the lifeguard hadn't got there first." No. It's always the dog food, and the Hendersons are therefore entitled to be in the vast circle of acquaintainces who go "Bowwow."

Another angle on this, there may be something that you are kind of proud of and that while you may not be the best at it you are among the Top Ten. Let's say you can crack your knuckles to the tune of "Yankee Doodle." Well, that's fine until you get to an age where you've got some distinguished gray at the temples and the whole image is pretty sedate and dignified.

Then just as you're telling some lovely lady about the inside story on Vietnam as you see it, a cry goes up for you to crack your knuckles to the tune of "Yankee Doodle."

You know, you're secretly pleased that people remember and that they want to hear you crack your knuckles to the tune of "Yankee Doodle." But you've done it so many times that you don't really pay attention, and as a result you make a little mistake and people say, "Well, he's washed up. I got a nine-year-old nephew can out-knuckle-crack him." And this from the same people who were urging you on and getting other people to come in from the porch and going, "Everybody hold the noise down and listen to this; it's fabulous."

Put this down as an indelible fact—the guy who is always pushing you to play the zither is the first one to spread it around that you are getting to be a pain in the neck the way you always drag out that tired old zither.

All the foregoing comes to mind with the annual call for me to pick the Kansas City Athletics to win the American League pennant. I had intended to pass it up this year; after all, a creative artist must grow. He is not like the sportswriter who can go on repeating the same things year after year.

I have been persuaded, however, that for me to eschew this annual rite would be like Judy Garland leaving "Somewhere Over the Rainbow" out of her repertoire. So, all right, the A's will take it all this year. It is my tenth straight prediction to this effect. And, as I said above, watch the very people who crowded me into making it be the first to snigger and say what a bore the old gent has become.

The trouble corn can cause

¶ I tend to worry about the political and economic opinions of a man who uses silver prongs while eating corn on the cob.

I have a brother I don't see much of, mainly because of the way he eats corn on the cob.

This is sort of hard to describe without hands, but what he did (and still does, for all I know) was start in at the left end of the cob and eat all the way around it, then move to the right, revolve the cob again, and so on.

Most people, most normal people—people like me, in other words—operate on the typewriter principle. We eat along a row of kernels, or two or three rows according to mouth size, then we hear the tinkle of a mental bell, and we shift the carriage back from right to left and start all over again.

Am I being at all clear about this?

To use a military figure, most corn eaters I have ever encountered eat along the ranks. My brother devoured the cob by files.

Does calling what I think of as the normal method of corn eating the longitudinal approach and my brother's system the latitudinal attack help any?

The difference, to make it absolutely translucent, is between the lateral and the revolving method of eating corn on the cob.

My brother may have been the first time-motion study man. If he had applied his bright ideas to making automobiles instead of eating corn on the cob, he would be in a position to do a little something for his relatives today.

But all he would do was eat corn on the cob in that silly, unnatural way he had thought up and justify it by claiming it was more efficient.

He said that the normal way of eating corn, the way Pocahontas taught Captain John Smith, the way George Washington would have eaten corn on the cob at Valley Forge if it hadn't been the dead of winter, was a waste of effort.

He said that using this silly system he thought up, you could keep your elbows planted on the table and eat a half, or anyway a third, of the ear just by twirling your fingers, and then you only had to make one simple little adjustment of your mouth and you had the next half (or third) all ready to eat.

He said that a lot that was wrong with the country was that people were wasting their time with the old-fashioned typewriter method of eating corn.

I used to answer him with withering sarcasm, such as "It is a good thing that the man who invented the typewriter didn't eat corn on the cob the way you do or we'd still be writing with the goose quill pen."

It didn't bother him.

To be perfectly frank, the reason it bothered me was that I suspected he was probably right—logically and scientifically.

I couldn't match his arguments; all I had was faith, a deep, inner conviction that, when it came to eating corn on the cob, I was right and he was wrong. The years have, I think, borne me out. In fact the victory for the straight-along-the-cob method of eating corn is so complete that I had been lulled into a sense of security.

Until the other night when I looked across the table at my little girl, who is, for the first time, showing a real interest in corn.

Do I have to tell you how she was eating it?

Once an odd bad strain gets into a family, it lasts for generations, as many a bald-headed, left-handed, blue-eyed fruit fly can testify.

The sins of the uncles . . .

Tennessee Williams, the playwright, says he is going to change his batting stance and write about something besides decadent Southerners—decadent Northerners, perhaps. I can sympathize with him. You write about something and suddenly everybody assumes that it's the only thing in life that interests you.

I guess everybody who had a little anecdote about Dixie decadence sent it in to old Tenn, and I can see how it would get tiresome.

Shakespeare had the same problem. He wrote one play about a melancholy Dane. And ever after, like when he might be sitting at his ease in the Mermaid Tavern, some guy would come over to his table, set down a flagon of wine and start telling melancholy Dane stories.

He got so bored with the whole thing that he called off a lot of sequels he had planned, such as *Hamlet Meets Antony and Cleopatra.*

Far be it from anybody I know to imply that I am in the same league with these two sluggers, but I know something of the problem.

When I attempted the essay on eating corn on the cob or roasting ears or whatever you want to call it, according to your folksiness quotient, I thought I was through with the subject.

Now I am known, in glittering salon or bustling marketplace, as a man with a deep, abiding dedication to research into corn-eating habits. My mail is cluttered with letters on the subject. Near strangers offer to demonstrate their own technique, if I will supply the corn.

So I think you will understand that it is with some apprehension that I hazard further comment on corn eating. I would not do so, except that tear- or possibly butter-stained communications are reaching me, indicating that more families than I had thought possible share a shameful secret.

The two methods of corn eating which I discussed in *op. cit.* at least had this to be said for them—they were neat. Apparently, however, there is a third school of corn eating which is on the increase and may even be attaining a majority status.

Its practitioners are the lungers. A civic leader in a Nebraska town is described by a close associate as a lunger.

"He lunges at the ear ferociously and at random, hit or miss, caring nothing for order or pattern," the horror-struck eyewitness reports. "It is impossible to tell the ear he has finished eating from the one he is working on."

An Illinois father (and corn grower) tells a similar painful story: "My son follows a razzle-dazzle approach, which he frankly admits to be purely opportunistic. He simply eats on the cob, up and down, sideways, T-formation, zigzag, according to the path of the melted butter and where the salt falls. But it must be admitted that he leaves the cob picked clean. My little girls, on the other hand, leave the ear very rough, with many divots of half-topped corn sticking up."

A Kansas lady's burden is a sister who "eats a gob here and a gob there. I can only describe this as the Grazing Cow attack."

Her sister, the lady continues, "claims it's a great thrill to look around the cob and discover one more delectable chomp when you'd swear you had finished."

(Aside from the subject, but of morbid interest, it might be recorded that this lady also has in her family a man who holds the corn by driving a screwdriver into one end of the cob, and another who butters the corn by first buttering a slice of bread and wrapping it around the ear. Later he eats the bread.)

Of course, the corn-on-the-cobber who insists on following the rows of kernels too meticulously is going to have a heck of a time with Country Gentleman corn, where the arrangement is rather random. Let us ignore that point as minor.

The fact is that this lunging, don't-give-a-darn, careless way of eating corn is a mark of declining standards, weakening of the moral fiber and a falling away from the great principles of order that rule the universe. It was saddening to discover that it is so widespread.

EPILOGUE

One source of the widespread dissatisfaction with books is the way they end. You are going along pretty good with the story and suddenly there is a flicker of blank pages like the unexposed frames at the end of a reel of film, and that is all.

You are left there with the book in your lap and half a drink unfinished. There is no letdown of this kind with a newspaper. The long analysis of the situation in Cambodia ends with a filler that tells you the Detroit Tigers will play 30 night games at home next season.

Or you can turn back and read "Proud of Her Big Petunia" or "Sees Banner Retail Year" or some other item from which you had been distracted by your passionate interest in Cambodian affairs.

In a book we miss that brief, finishing canter at the end of the race which Justice Oliver Wendell Holmes said is an essential part of life.

The old novelists realized this. They gave us an epilogue or a postlude along these lines: "The reader may be interested in learning that, since the painful scene on the quay at Marseilles, our dear, old friend, Dobbins, has been comfortably installed with little Nancy in the dear, old cottage at Wapley-on-the-Souse. I regret to say that, in his anger over losing the deed to the Saucy Belle, Squire Quimby died of apoplexy, thereby leaving Big Tim free to marry Middle-Size Sue."

This sort of thing no longer goes. About the only kind of acceptable epilogue for a book these days is the "Note on the Type in Which This Book Is Printed."

It has sustained me in many a difficult time. I have finished a book. It ends with a clang, as though a portcullis had fallen: Norris is going to try to get along better at the advertising agency and Sheila takes Norval back, weak though he is. But it's still half an hour until the airplane lands. That's when I appreciate the note that tells me the book has been set in 10-point Caslon on a 12-point slug. I turn to the scene where Sheila reaches over to the bedside table and gets a cigarette which she lights and hands to Norris.

"Son of a gun," I say to myself. "It's Caslon Old Style all right."

I may show it to my charming seatmate and say, "Some Caslon Old Style, hey, kid?"

I would like to provide information like that about this book, but to tell you the truth I don't know whether it's Bodoni Bare-face or Gutenberg Congealed. What I think we did, as a matter of fact, was call in different men for each letter.

I don't like the capital-E specialist. He has that middle little spike shorter than the other two. I personally prefer the middle little spike to be the longest one. The Greek idea of beauty was that a lady's No. 2 toe should be longer than her big toe. Be that as it may; I am not a toe man, but I know what I like in capital E's.

Nor do I care too much for the lower-case a. Its belly sags. My apologies to the type foundry, but it's got a bad small a there.

On the plus side, the top big Q consultant jetted in from the Coast and did a simply fantastic job. I went back over the proofs and put in three more capital-Q words to take advantage of his artistry.

    I realize that typographers are just as sensitive as anyone else. I warned the magazine designers that no good would come of crowding the *Saturday Evening* inside the *O* of *Post,* but they went ahead, and the only thing I hear from Philadelphia any more is silence.

    So it may be that I have offended the type people in this epilogue. If so, I am sorry I stirred it. All I was trying to do was give us that last little bit of reading before the nurse comes around and asks us, "Are we ready to turn out our light?"

ABOUT THE AUTHOR

BILL VAUGHAN was born upstairs over a St. Louis drugstore[1] in 1915. He went to Washington University[2] where only an aversion for quantitative analysis[3] kept him from becoming a celebrated doctor[4] instead of a celebrated newspaperman.[5] He started his career as Inquiring Reporter[6] in Springfield, Mo., then moved to the *Kansas City Star* where his paragraphs[7] and columns have tickled a devoted public for twenty-five years. He has also added at least one footnote to history.[8] His ephemeral art would have been forever buried in musty newspaper files had not a wise and kindly Publisher[9] collected his finest pieces for posterity between the covers of a book. Immediately thousands of exceptionally nice people were given the bird;[10] and as this goes to press, first advance readers of his new book are already stir-crazy.[11]

---

1   At the corner of Skinker and Delmar.

2   *Not* the one in Seattle. Why would he go to Seattle when there's a perfectly good one in St. Louis?

3   "You were supposed to analyze what was in bottles, but I figured that real-life bottles come with labels telling what's in them."

4   Like his father, grandfather, granduncle and elder brother Russell.

5   He's syndicated in 115 papers including 7 abroad: so he *must* be celebrated.

6   "I wasn't cut out for it. I always did hate having to ask people questions about things that were none of my business."

7   "So rare is the professional paragrapher* that Vaughan is occasionally credited with being the last of the breed. He is not.** But he is probably the best of a tiny handful of newsmen who still work at the art of polishing a line or two of type*** until it gleams."—*Time.*

8   Vaughan decided that President Millard Fillmore needed boosting, so he wrote that Fillmore had encouraged Morse to invent the telegraph, and that, out of gratitude, Morse named his code characters Dot and Dash after Fillmore's children, Dorothy and Dashiell. This has since been widely published as perfectly straight statement of historical fact.

9   Who but Essandess?

10 *Bird Thou Never Wert*, Bill Vaughan's first book.

11 I.e., crazy over *Sorry I Stirred It.*

---

* "We used to roam the prairies like the buffalo and the antelope, in vast herds as far as the eye could see."

** "But today there are only a few moth-eaten examples of us left."

*** "You have to say something wise or funny in 25 or 30 words, with no padding to conceal the lack of point."

CHRISTIAN COLLEGE LIBRARY
COLUMBIA, MISSOURI